MASTERING MANAGEMENT CONSULTANCY

Calvert Markham

Legend Business Ltd,
107-111 Fleet Street, London, EC4A 2AB
info@legend-paperbooks.co.uk | www.legendpress.co.uk

Contents © Calvert Markham 2019
The right of the above author to be identified as the author of this work has been asserted in accordance with the Copyright, Designs and Patents Act 1988. British Library Cataloguing in Publication Data available.

Print ISBN 9781789550795
Ebook ISBN 9781789550801
Set in Times. Printing managed by Jellyfish Solutions Ltd
Cover design by Simon Levy | www.simonlevyassociates.co.uk

Publishers Note
Every possible effort has been made to ensure that the information contained in this book is accurate at the time of going to press, and the publisher and author cannot accept responsibility for any errors or omissions, however caused. No responsibility for loss or damage occasioned to any person acting, or refraining from action, as a result of the material in this publication can be accepted by the editor, the publisher or any of the authors.

All rights reserved. No part of this publication may be reproduced, stored in or introduced into a retrieval system, or transmitted, in any form, or by any means electronic, mechanical, photocopying, recording or otherwise, without the prior permission of the publisher. Any person who commits any unauthorised act in relation to this publication may be liable to criminal prosecution and civil claims for damages.

CONTENTS

Preface 7

Introduction 8

1 The nature of consultancy 9
    What is consultancy? 9
    Why use consultants? 11
    The nature of consultancy practices 12
    The role of the consultant 14
    What sort of people become consultants? 15
    The relationship between the practice and the client 16
    Consultancy skills 16

2 Consultancy problem solving 18
    The structure of business problems 19
    Making sense of a client's predicament 22
    The problem solving approach 32
    Data collection 37
    Data analysis and conclusions 45

3 Operating a consultancy project 48
    The structure of a consultancy project 48
    Terms of reference specify the project 51
    Diagnosis: managing consultancy projects 63
    Intervention: developing and implementing recommendations 67
    Closure: completing the project 75

4 Managing client relationships 77
    Why the client relationship is important 78
    Account management 80

Factors contributing to the quality of a relationship 84
Monitoring the client relationship 90
Creating satisfied clients 92

5 Product definition and marketing in consultancy 97
Product-market definition 98
Marketing consultancy 102
Promotional activities 106

6 The consultancy sales process 108
The consultancy sales process 109
Relationship development 110
Prospection 114
Developing the proposition 115
Pitching for the sale 117
Organising for selling 119
Monitoring sales performance 122
Developing sales performance 126

7 Conducting specific sales transactions 128
Becoming a consultancy salesperson 128
The ingredients of selling performance 131
Purposes of selling – what we are trying to achieve 132
The sales process 136
Establishing a dialogue with a prospective client 137
Conducting selling transactions 140
Converting the ITT to a sale 149
Developing selling skills 153

8 Commercial aspects of consultancy 161
Determining fee rates 161
Expenses 163
What do we tell the client? 164
Terms of payment 166
Other methods of generating revenue in consultancy 170
Using sub-contractors 172
Non-time related charges 172
Terms of business 173

9 Managing a consultancy business 177
　　Leadership in a consultancy practice 178
　　Organisation structure within a consultancy practice 179
　　Intellectual property in a consultancy practice 182
　　Managing consultants 184

Epilogue 191

Publishing history
As **The Top Consultant**
First edition 1993
Second edition 1994
Third edition 1998
Third revised edition 2001
Fourth edition 2004
Fifth edition 2014
As **Mastering Management Consultancy**
Sixth edition 2019
ISBN: 978-0-7494 4253 8

PREFACE

'Management Consultant' was an unusual occupation when I started my career but nowadays consultancy is a commonplace activity. Many will see a spell as a consultant as an essential ingredient of a well-rounded CV before moving into an executive position, while others, like me, have made a career of it. Latterly those in internal support functions (such as HR and IT) have also been encouraged to take on consultancy roles, while line managers, too, increasingly need to introduce discontinuous change, demanding a measure of consultancy skills.

Likewise, much has changed in the world of consultancy in the years since the first publication of this book as has my role, as at the time of this publication I am currently Director of the Centre for Management Consulting Excellence. Early in 2019 the Centre published research into the skills that are thought to be needed by management consultants in 2030 and these highlighted the need for technical skills in areas that would have been unthought of at the time of the first edition of this book. But the research also noted that there are timeless skills that management consultants have needed in the past and will continue to need in the future: how best to engage with clients to sell and deliver your consulting services; how to manage consulting as a business; how best to invest your time in conducting a consulting project; how to keep your clients happy. Although the context may have changed, it is these perennial issues that this book addresses.

Calvert Markham
July 2019

INTRODUCTION

Consultancy requires skills in selling and delivering services to clients and in running a consultancy business and this book addresses these topics. Commercial and business management responsibilities are likely to be undertaken by more experienced consultants in larger practices arriving through a process of career progression, although sole practitioners need to consider them from the outset.

In this book we start with a definition of consultancy and the following chapters follow the likely career progression of a management consultant.

All consultants are engaged in delivering consulting services to their clients and so we start with the skills involved in this. While some consulting work consists of simply giving advice – the situation where a client has a question and the consultant knows the answer – most of the work involves some investigation in order to define and solve a problem, so we start with problem solving. Problem solving needs to be embodied in a consulting process, which gives shape to a consulting project, so that is the next topic dealt with. This work needs to be done within a client environment, and so the third chapter in this section is devoted to managing client relationships.

As their career progresses, a consultant will be required to take on commercial responsibilities. The chapters dealing with this cover marketing and sales and also the commercial aspects of arriving at a deal with a client.

Finally, consultancy has to be delivered within a business organisation and so we finish by looking at some of the considerations that need to be given to the organisation and management of a consulting practice.

Whatever your role, I hope that you will find ideas and techniques in this book that will enable you to develop your performance in mastering management consultancy.

1
THE NATURE OF CONSULTANCY

One hundred years ago the management consultancy industry did not exist; now, consultancy is globally a multi-billion dollar industry, covering many service lines in addition to advice to management. Organisations have in recent years increasingly outsourced more peripheral activities and consultancy firms have responded with an expanding range of services.

Now, consultancy firms have expanded to include thousands of consultants handling large-scale projects and process outsourcing activities, while at the same time there is a horde of sole practitioners and small firms delivering more modest consultancy services to their clients. So, what is this consultancy business?

In this chapter we will consider what consultancy is, why consultants are engaged, the nature of the organisations delivering consultancy services, and the skills required of consultants.

WHAT IS CONSULTANCY?

One of my first assignments as a management consultant was with one of the London teaching hospitals. I heard that a colleague was a patient in one of the wards and I wanted to know which one, so I phoned the appropriate department. Information was given only reluctantly over the phone, until I was asked who I was. 'I'm a consultant and she's a member of my firm,' I replied, honestly. There was a sound of clicking heels as the person at the other end of the phone came to attention – and I got the information I wanted immediately. 'Consultant' and 'firm' then had quite different (and more potent) meanings in a hospital.

At one extreme the term 'consultant' simply refers to the nature of engagement between an individual and an organisation; the consultant is a person who is acting in a contracted rather than an employed capacity. Beyond this, the word is applied in a variety of occupations; as well as the senior doctor and the management consultant, it can be used to describe anybody who is providing knowledge-based services to an organisation from outside. So a wider definition of the term 'consultant' could also include solicitor, accountant, architect, engineer or, indeed, any profession.

A simple definition of consultancy is 'delivering specialist skills in a client environment'. Key concepts in this definition are:

- *Specialist skills:* The assumption is that the consultant has specific skills, both in demand and valued by the client organisation, and it is for this reason that the individual consultant has been engaged.
- *Outside the organisation:* The consultant is usually from another organisation or, if an internal consultant, from a different department within the organisation. This has been extended to the concept of 'business partner' – an internal service provider (for example, from the HR department) who has been assigned to a business unit to work in a consultative capacity with them – who also needs consulting skills.

Although any provider of professional services might be regarded as a consultant (and their methods of winning business and handling clients will have much in common), the matters on which *management* consultants are engaged are around helping organisations define and implement their development agendas. The development agenda is not only about doing new things, but also about doing existing things better.

The nature of management consultancy interventions has evolved, as shown in Exhibit 1.1. As the diagram shows, consultants can be involved at a number of levels:

Exhibit 1.1 Evolution of activities in a consultancy practice

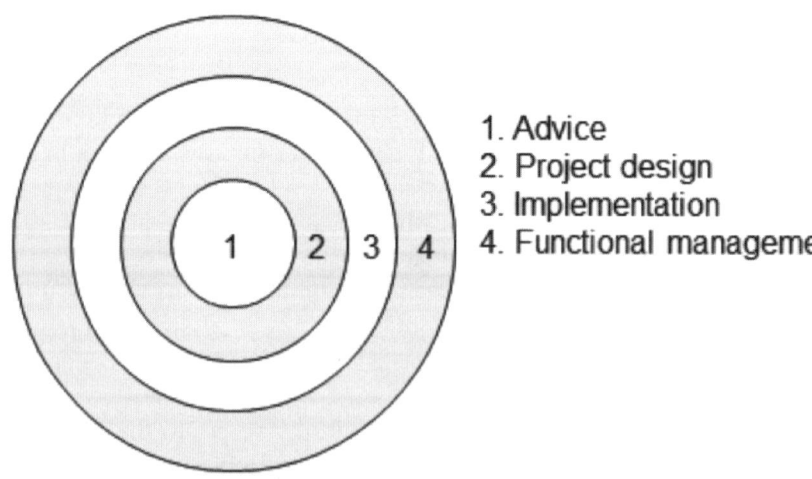

1. Advice
2. Project design
3. Implementation
4. Functional management

Providing advice: This work might answer a question such as: "What is the reward package needed to attract a good marketing manager?"
Project design goes a step further, answering a question such as: "How do we ensure that our reward packages remain competitive?"
Implementation goes a step still further: "Install a new reward system for this business that gives better value for money".
Functional management takes on running a complete function: "Please run our reward system on our behalf".

Each stage represents an increased level of outsourcing and a larger 'footprint' for the consultancy practice in the client organisation. For example, an HR manager may be charged with managing a company reward system and decide to initiate a project to ensure that reward remains competitive, enlisting the help of consultants to design this (level 2), which she then implements (level 3). These steps therefore represent an evolving degree towards 'buy' in terms of a strategic 'make or buy' decision.

WHY USE CONSULTANTS?

All organisations have suppliers – of utilities, raw materials and so on. Organisations need to decide what they should source internally and what they should buy in the 'make or buy' decision.

The structure of business has changed radically over the last 30 years: whereas large corporations would have had teams of in-house specialists to help with projects as and when required, the consequence of successive cost cutting exercises has been that many specialist departments have closed. Specialist expertise is now externally resourced – not only in consultancy and other professions, but also in many other areas – for example, office cleaning, running canteens and security. Activities that are not vital to the core of the business are sub-contracted and there are now many very large businesses that have flourished because of this trend.

So the principle of using specialist outsiders is established. The next question is: on what activities should they be engaged?

The obvious answer is where organisations do not have the quality or quantity of resource to achieve the results desired. A simple analogy: you want to replace the central heating system in your house; if you do not know how to do this, you will probably engage a plumber to do it for you. Or, you may be able to do it, but have insufficient time to do so, in which case you would again sub-contract the work.

There are three other factors that organisations may also take into consideration in deciding whether to sub-contract:

1. *Objectivity*: Will insiders bring the independence and freshness of view that an outsider would bring?
2. *Risk*: Bringing in outside experts should mitigate the risks of the project failing (and, if you are cynical, will provide an obvious scapegoat if it does!)
3. *Learning,* in which there are two questions to consider:
   - How will our organisational knowledge be increased as a result of using consultants and learning from them?
   - What opportunities for learning among our own people will be lost by engaging outside consultants?

Taking the central heating analogy above, for example, you may wish to work alongside the plumber if you want to learn how to install central heating systems for yourself in future. But how often would you expect to need to do this? Would it be a worthwhile investment of your time that would lead to future benefit?

These factors are also relevant to the use of internal consultants. The value of establishing an internal consultancy practice is that it allows the development of a centre of excellence in an area of specialist activity that would not be economically viable if diffused throughout an organisation. Moreover, leading-edge practice is not always available from external consultancies. Organisations may be able to acquire learning and capability in areas relevant to their business more easily than consultants. In many situations a joint client-consultant team can therefore be very effective.

THE NATURE OF CONSULTANCY PRACTICES

There are clear benefits in consultants associating. Quite apart from the economies of scale in sharing administrative overheads, there is far more likelihood that the right blend of skills to address clients' issues will be available from a group of consultants than from a sole practitioner.

There are two major tasks in consultancy, both of which take time: acquiring engagements, and executing them. Exhibit 1.2 shows how consultants can leverage the two resources required to carry these out – their network of client contacts, and their specialist skills.

Associations of consultants can vary from a loose network through to a formally constituted practice. The latter will have a well-developed infrastructure with consultants trained in using shared procedures, based on capabilities derived from accumulated corporate experience when working with clients. In recent years large consultancy practices have flourished, developing on a global basis and taking on massive projects, either by themselves or as part of a consortium, the latter often involving partners from quite different kinds of business.

Exhibit 1.2 Consultants in combination can better win and operate assignments

Who has the client relationship?		Who has the capability?	
		Me	Others
Others		Alliances leveraging off others' client relationships	Consultancy firm
Me		Sole practitioner	Alliances utilising others' capabilities

Muzio, Kirkpatrick, and Kipping have suggested that consulting has proceeded as a series of three waves, and suggested a look to the future in a fourth. They have typified the first three respectively – which have developed over the last 100 years – as Engineers, Strategists and IT Integrators, with characteristics as follows:

First wave: Engineers	<ul><li>Application of scientific management to improve work-flow and production processes</li><li>Level of intervention: shop floor</li><li>Engineering knowledge-base and background</li><li>Flat structures and charismatic authority</li><li>Federations of national entities</li><li>High levels of autonomy</li></ul>
Second wave: Strategists	<ul><li>Provide high level advice on strategic issues</li><li>Level of intervention: corporate headquarters</li><li>Development of proprietary management methodologies, frameworks and techniques</li><li>Reliance on MBA graduates</li><li>Collegiality and partnership</li><li>Moderate leverage, team work, up or out culture</li><li>Personalisation strategies</li></ul>
Third wave: IT Integrators	<ul><li>Deal with ICT requirements of increasingly networked forms of organisations</li><li>IT focused/driven advice</li><li>Level of intervention: relationships between firms and units</li><li>Integration of advice and implementation</li></ul>

- Part of broader professional service firms or standalone listed corporations
- Bureaucracy, standardised patterns of activity, developed managerial processes and structures
- High leverage ratios, developed hierarchies and codification strategies
- Graduate recruitment. Reliance on corporate training and internal labour markets

They further distinguish their attitudes to professionalism thus:
- *The First Wave*: Reliance on engineering qualifications, values and institutions.
- *The Second Wave*: Symbolic approach to professionalism and the mimicking of the outward appearance and discourse of established professions (especially law).
- *The Third Wave*: Development of corporate versions of professionalism based on internal standards, codes and qualifications.

And what of the Fourth Wave? The authors point to new forms of specialist/niche services (e.g. environmental consultancy); amalgamation within broader professional services firms (the one stop shop); and development of virtual forms of organisation and delivery (project based organisations). These of course are quite common in other industries – for example, in the film making industry, where a team of specialists are brought together to make a film, but have no commitment to work together again thereafter.

THE ROLE OF THE CONSULTANT

The role of the consultant within the consultancy practice has also evolved over the last 30 years. Certainly within my consultancy life it has evolved from being navigational, guiding the client's own staff to do the work themselves, to being substitutional, taking on a lot of the work that previously might have been done by client staff. Now we can see several roles for consultants:
- The consultant as the conduit through which the specialist knowledge of a practice is transmitted. Management consultancies' 'products' consist of well-tried services or methodologies; the theory and practice of their introduction is incorporated in manuals and consultants trained in their application.
- The consultant as 'management mercenary'. The consultant is a generalist, perhaps with an MBA or some similar qualification. Their role is that of a gun for hire – a bright trouble-shooter who can take a

new problem and resolve it from first principles. Previous experience is not essential; what is offered is a superior skill.
- The consultant as specialist. The consultant is hired because of the relevance of their skills to the problem in hand. Previous experience and personal expertise are important, but must be complemented with a capability to deliver specialist skills in a client environment.

Of course, these roles not only overlap but also are not exclusive.

A feature of the roles described above is that clients hire not only a consultancy *per se* but also assess the people in the consultancy. Clients have become more discerning and may not simply rely on the reputation of the practice but may also want to vet the quality of the consultants put forward. It is therefore worth considering the provenance of people who become management consultants.

WHAT SORT OF PEOPLE BECOME CONSULTANTS?

Many people become consultants having previously worked in specialist line positions. Indeed, management consultancies often draw their recruits from this source and develop them by training and supervision in the skills required of a consultant.

Other specialists have chosen to become freelance consultants because they have been made redundant or taken early retirement. For many in this group, the notion of consultancy is not about the professional skills involved but more about their commercial relationship with those who are paying them; they are no longer employees, but self-employed contractors. Some will continue to confine their role to specialist sub-contractor, while others will develop consultancy skills. Indeed some large organisations have set up consulting subsidiaries as a means of retaining access to skills of those who might otherwise have left.

For those in a consultancy practice, there is a choice of role. Consultants can be simply the trained providers of a proprietary product or promoted as experts in their own right. Each approach has advantages and disadvantages. The practice with proprietary consultancy approaches will presumably market them as such, so a newcomer to the market has therefore not only to develop a new approach, and to prove that it is workable, but also to challenge the brand of the established provider. By contrast, if the consultancy product is vested in the skills of an individual consultant, it is easy for the specialist to leave this employment and take their skills – and possibly clients – to another employer, or set up their own consultancy business. This is of course how some of even the most venerable of the consultancies in the UK were started.

THE RELATIONSHIP BETWEEN THE PRACTICE AND THE CLIENT

At one extreme the relationship between the consultancy practice and the client is arms-length; the consultancy is employed on a one-off basis to meet a specific need that the client is unable to meet from their own resources. At the other extreme there is an almost symbiotic relationship: the consultancy has been selected not only because of the value it can add to the client's business, but also because they feel comfortable doing business together; there is a good cultural match.

With the evolution mentioned earlier, so too has the typical relationship between consultancy practice and client developed, from the arms-length sale to the alliance based on a long-term mutual benefit.

Not all relationships between consultancies and their clients will be this close, of course; at the start, many will be on an arms-length basis, anyway. The important point is that there has been a change in mindset; a consultancy is not engaged in just a sale: it is developing an alliance. Long-term considerations apply, rather than just those relating to the immediate transaction with the client.

Again, the growth of the consultancy business means that it is quite possible that a senior executive commissioning a consultancy project may have had a period of experience as a consultant (or will have worked with consultants before) and will be familiar with the techniques of selling and operating consultancy projects. Clients have matured in their evaluation of the consultancy offering. This means that there is now a larger measure of equality between consultants and their clients.

CONSULTANCY SKILLS

There are three components to consultancy skills:
- The *body of knowledge, skills and experience* which the consultant has on offer. This might be civil engineering, tax law, software applications or whatever the consultant purports to be expert in.
- Experience or knowledge of *the application of the specialist skill to a specific area*. This might be, for example, an industrial sector, a geographical area, or a particular type of problem.
- *Consultancy skills*, which enable the consultant to deliver their expertise within the client environment.

These three components are like the legs of a three-legged stool: all have to be present if a consultant is to carry out the role effectively. If one leg is missing, the stool is at best wobbly and at worst falls over.

This book concentrates on the third component – the skills required to engage in consultancy, which are necessary irrespective of the specialist expertise of the individual or the area of its application.

The skills can be divided into two:
1. Those relating to business aspects of consultancy: product development and marketing; the sales process and how to manage it; commercial aspects of dealing with clients; and managing the business as a whole.
2. Those needed to conduct these tasks well: how to sell; problem solving; operating consultancy projects; and managing client relationships throughout.

There is overlap between all these topics. But the message that the reader should take away is that it is not sufficient simply to have knowledge to be effective as a consultant: there are real skills needed as well – and these are the burden of this book.

2

CONSULTANCY PROBLEM SOLVING

In Windsor Great Park there is a path, or more accurately an avenue, called the Long Walk. Extending for three miles in a straight line, it passes through the park towards Windsor Castle. The path is wide – you can wander within its limits, but its boundaries are clear, and, as you walk along it, the prospect of the Castle is always in view.

Some consultancy projects are like that path and are conducted by using a standardised approach. From start to finish the path – the series of tasks required to conduct the project – is clear. There may be minor deviations along the way but these will be within the broad boundaries. The outcome will be as clearly in sight as Windsor Castle.

By contrast, there are other consultancy projects that are forays into unknown territory. Like the search for El Dorado – a fabulous city in South America sought by explorers five hundred years ago – these projects seek a goal that is believed to exist but its detailed nature, its location and the path there are uncertain. Such projects are needed when unprecedented or peculiar problems (often called 'messy' or 'wicked') have to be addressed. As with a journey into the unknown, it is easy on these projects to lose your way; to take wrong turnings; to waste time; to fail to meet the goal. But first you must recognise that you have to deal with a messy problem. The consultant unaware of this is like the young army officer, whose colonel wrote of him, 'Undoubtedly there are soldiers who would follow this officer but, if so, it would be only out of a sense of curiosity to find out where he was going.'

There is a poem about 6 blind men encountering an elephant for the first time. Each feels a different part of the elephant – hide, tusks, trunk, legs etc. – and confidently asserts (quite wrongly), the properties of an elephant based on his limited information.

Organisations are like the elephant and those of us who engage with them are like the blind men; at best we have a partial view. If you take a systems view of an organisation, everything is connected to everything else. You have therefore to define some boundaries to the area of your study, otherwise you will be faced with an impossibly complex task in addressing any organisational issue.

The challenge for the consultant is where to draw the boundaries; focus on the wrong area and your intervention may be ineffective. Moreover, you need to be sure that what you are proposing is 'do-able' – that in effect you are not trying to boil the ocean.

The challenge is depicted in Exhibit 2.1: clients are faced with many predicaments but well defined, time and resource bounded projects are designed by consultants to address them. Of course, there will rarely be a perfect fit between predicament and project, but the quality of fit will be a function of how well the consultant understands the client's situation and designs an appropriate approach. It is this skill which this chapter addresses.

Exhibit 2.1 The critical skill of projectising

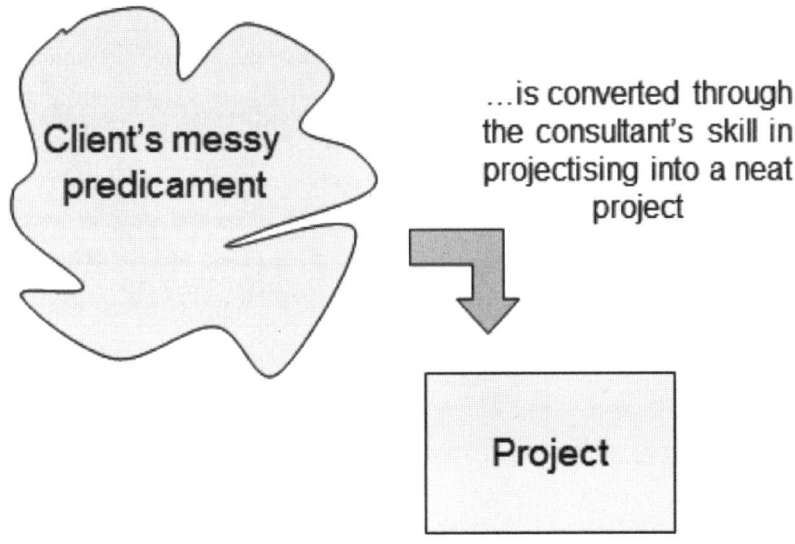

THE STRUCTURE OF BUSINESS PROBLEMS

A simple model of a business organisation is illustrated in Exhibit 2.2.

Top management is preoccupied with the direction of an organisation – its strategy; middle management is preoccupied with the design of the infrastructure that enables the strategy to be achieved – process design and

Exhibit 2.2 A simple model of business organisation

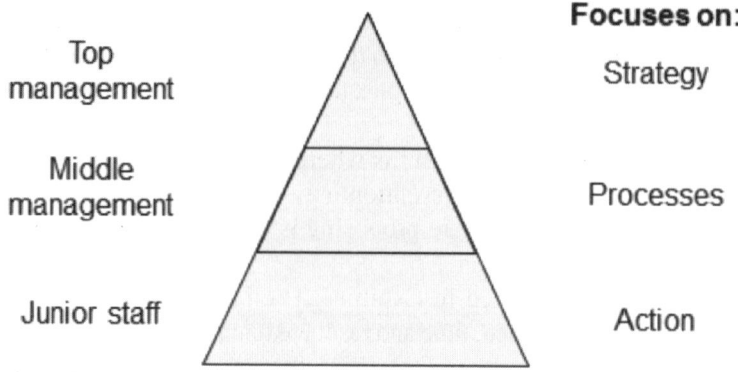

operation. Junior staff take action within this framework. Consultants may assist at all levels, but all three are interdependent. In particular, processes can be defined only in the context of a strategy, whilst activity has to be within the process framework – the level above creates boundaries, except in the case of strategy. (Incidentally, I am giving a broad definition here of strategy.)

The consultants who engage at these three levels can be designated strategic, functional, and technical, and the characteristics of the problem in which they engage are shown in Exhibit 2.3.

Exhibit 2.3 Consultants and problems

Organisational concern	Type of consultant	Type of problem
Strategy	Strategic	Many degrees of freedom; problems ill defined; solutions unbounded
Process	Functional	
Action	Technical	Few degrees of freedom; problems well defined, solutions bounded

THE VARIETY OF CONSULTANCY PROBLEMS

Technical consultancy is not confined to technology, but also includes consultancy that is carried out by specialists applying standard techniques, for example:
- a recruitment consultant, finding a suitable candidate to fill a job vacancy;
- an accountant advising on a company's tax affairs;
- an IT consultant, advising on the choice of computer system.

On the whole, questions are easier to identify and the answers easier to define at the technical level. For example, a recruitment consultant may be retained to find a candidate for the position of Marketing Director for a client. The question is clear; so too are the features of the answer – the consultant needs to provide the client with a shortlist of suitable, qualified candidates.

Problem solving consists of the process to be followed leading to the answer. In the case of recruitment, the process might follow the sequence shown below.

1. Get a job description for new position.
2. Identify key aspects of business and environment in which the new appointee will be working.
3. Determine contents of remuneration package and scope for negotiation.
4. Agree person specification with client.
5. Agree an advertising campaign and copy to be used.
6. Place adverts.
7. Sort responses. Identify long list for interview.
8. Interview and identify suitable candidates.
9. Provide client with shortlist of names and reports on each.

This is a clear process, akin to the Long Walk described at the start of this chapter. By contrast, the questions and answers responding to a client predicament around, say, 'How should we engage best with Western Pacific economies?' are much more like the hunt for El Dorado. But equally, a process is needed to engage with these types of problems.

Of course, technical consultants will seek to reassure themselves of the soundness of the assumptions underpinning their project. Thus, in the examples above:

- a recruitment consultant will want to understand the current operations of a business and how it is likely to develop, before advising on the recruitment of a senior executive;
- an accountant will need to understand the corporate structure and how it might change before advising on optimising tax affairs;
- an IT consultant will need to know how the requirements of a business are likely to develop before advising on the choice of computer systems and software.

If a client cannot provide satisfactory answers to these questions, there may be functional or strategic consultancy work that needs to be done before a project in a technical area can proceed. Sometimes consultants are accused of commercial opportunism, setting out to enlarge the scope of their projects beyond those set by clients, whereas in fact extra work is required to provide a sufficiently sound basis for the original project to proceed. Indeed, it is usually good practice for a consultant to be at least thinking, if not working, at a degree of freedom beyond that set by the client's thinking.

For example, a multinational firm was considering reviewing the remuneration packages of its top 200 or so executives. Some worked in subsidiary companies and some at head office, but all were treated for remuneration purposes as a single executive cadre. The consultant looked into the business and personnel policies used by the client and discovered that:
- only rarely did an executive move from one subsidiary to another;
- the subsidiaries were largely autonomous – they did not depend on one another.

The executive cadre was a myth; there was no need for it. Thereafter, each executive was dealt with according to the subsidiary they worked for; the only 'executive cadre' was at corporate headquarters. The consultant had, necessarily, extended the scope of the brief to include issues of personnel policy so as to deal with the remuneration review satisfactorily.

This example illustrates the value of thinking at a degree of freedom greater than that of the client. The 'levels of intervention' model described below is a useful framework for doing this.

MAKING SENSE OF A CLIENT'S PREDICAMENT

It has sometimes been said that a consultant decides the answer to the client's problem on Day 2 of the project and spends the rest of the project proving it. If it proves not to be the case, then they go back again and choose another answer and check to see whether works.

This type of approach may work with simple problems but it is of limited value when dealing with messy problems. It relies on the consultant's preconceptions, and allows little scope for creativity. By contrast, a consultancy problem solving process for addressing messy problems must recognise that preconceptions inevitably exist and engage with them constructively.

RECOGNISING PRECONCEPTIONS

It is inevitable that the parties to a consultancy project bring preconceptions that are fashioned by their assumptions. Your judgement about what is relevant in a given situation, for example, will be a function of the skills, knowledge and experience relating to your expertise and its application. Plainly, it is neither possible nor appropriate to try to eliminate expert judgement from consultancy projects. But when entering on any consultancy project – particularly one of any complexity – it is sensible to examine the preconceptions of both consultant and client to see whether they are valid.

For example, a firm of solicitors decided that it wanted to improve the quality of its client service. It therefore engaged consultants to design and run a training course for all staff, which emphasised the importance of good quality client service and suggested how it might be developed.

In the event, the programme failed to improve the quality of client service because of the different preconceptions of the consultants and the solicitors:

- Each had clear, but different, views of what constituted good client service.
- The consultancy had previously provided similar training elsewhere, so assumed that this would be an appropriate method with this firm of solicitors.
- The solicitors took the view that training would be sufficient alone. The consultants failed to challenge this. What was needed in practice, however, was a framework in which people who had received the training could apply it.

Whenever a client and consultant come together, each will have some preconceptions relating to the prospective project. In the example above, consultant and client had similar preconceptions; had these been challenged, a better performance development programme should have resulted.

In other cases, their preconceptions may be different. For example, a consultant may have an idealised view of how a business such as the client's should work and base their diagnosis on a comparison of what is going on with that of an ideal. By contrast, the client may see the work required of the consultant entirely in terms of alleviating symptoms.

There are dangers with both perspectives; these can be illustrated by an analogy with a visit to a doctor. Suppose you visit your doctor because you have a stomach pain; here, the doctor is in the role of consultant, and you are the client. Taking an idealised view, the doctor might carry out an examination and say, 'I'm afraid you're a little overweight, and you have some skin blemishes. Your eyesight and hearing are not as good as they might be, and you look pretty unfit.'

All this may be true, but none of it is about your stomach pain. A consultant's diagnosis based on a comparison with an ideal will be equally unhelpful to a client.

On the other hand, you would not think much of a doctor who simply gave you tablets to take away the stomach pain, without bothering to examine you to find the cause. The treatment may alleviate the symptoms, but not deal with the underlying problem. For similar reasons, consultants should not confine their interventions to dealing only with the symptoms a client reports. Of course, as with a visit to a doctor, a client will describe the symptoms at the outset, but these should provide simply the starting point for the consultancy engagement.

So it is inevitable that both client and consultant will have preconceptions about a problem when they start work together. That they are preconceptions does not automatically invalidate them, however. A problem solving process should therefore:

- recognise that preconceptions exist and that they may have value;
- provide for them to be challenged where necessary.

DEVELOPING AN UNDERSTANDING OF THE CLIENT'S SITUATION

Exhibit 2.4 shows the structure by which the thinking of client and consultant can be progressed. This approach is an essential one in developing an understanding of the client's situation.

Exhibit 2.4: Progressive precision of specification

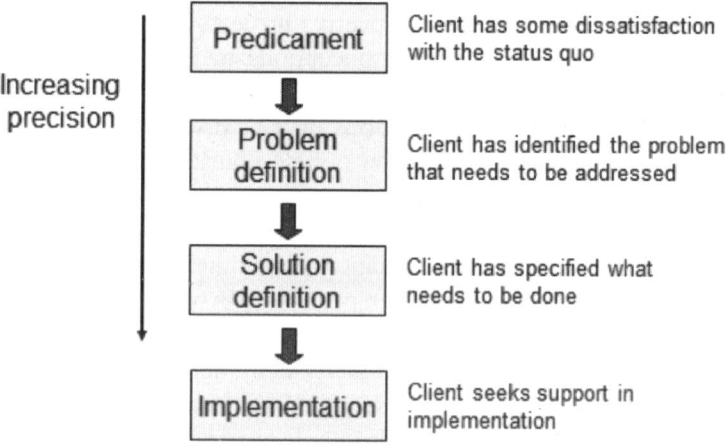

There is a structured method to understanding a client's situation, which can be best illustrated by a simple case study: International Cutlery Company (ICC), which is set out below.

> John Smith, a consultant, had been invited by the General Manager of the International Cutlery Company to tender for a project for reducing the cost of producing cutlery. 'Our competitors seem to be able to produce it for a lot less than we can – and I want to get our costs down to the same level as theirs,' the General Manager explained when Smith met him.

The business was a small subsidiary of Armfather Industries. As he showed Smith round the factory, the General Manager explained what was going on. In one corner, a group of operatives were sitting around laughing and chatting. The General Manager explained, 'They work on the "C" production line; they're having to wait while an engineer fixes the packaging machine.'

Quality control was very interesting; a large number of pieces of cutlery that did not meet specification had been placed in two piles. 'One pile are those which can easily be put right,' explained the quality inspector. 'Those others are a dead loss – they could never be fixed.' Smith asked whether the rejects were the result of the week's production so far.

'Goodness, no,' exclaimed the Inspector. 'These are just this morning's.'

The General Manager grumbled as they left. 'That means more overtime. Overtime costs are high enough as it is!'

Just as they reached the finishing shop, the General Manager's PA rushed up to them. 'I'm so glad to have caught you,' she said to him. 'Robinsons are on the line; they want to fix lunch sometime so that they can go over next year's prices with you.'

'I'd better talk to them,' said the General Manager 'Can you excuse me whilst I pop back to my office for five minutes? Robinsons are our major suppliers,' he went on to explain, before he left. 'They produce first class stuff, and their deliveries are always spot on. But, they really charge for it! That meeting is to discuss the price increase they're proposing for next year.'

John Smith went on into the finishing shop with the supervisor who had been hovering in the background since he had walked in with the General Manager. They chatted about the different qualities of finish various customers required. One interesting thing he learned was that most of the specifications had not changed at all over the last five years.

ISSUE ANALYSIS

The first step when faced with the situation described in the case study is to identify what the issues are. An issue can be prefaced with the phrase, 'I'm worried about...' Issue analysis consists of listing these worries.

At the end of his visit, therefore, John Smith might say, based on his observations:

'I'm worried about:
- wastage and rework rates;
- machine downtime;
- operative waiting time;
- customer expectations of quality;

- overtime costs;
- suppliers' prices'.

Based on his previous experience, he might add other issues to this list – for example:
'I'm worried about:
- the manning levels;
- work methods used;
- levels of stocks'.

None of these last three points can be inferred directly from the evidence given in the case study; John Smith has added them because of his specialised knowledge.

At this stage, these issues are only conjectural; John Smith does not know whether they are substantive or not. For example, by chance he may have arrived on the only day there has been a machine breakdown in five years, and so machine downtime would not be a major cause of uncompetitive productivity.

John Smith might also identify issues that are not related to the General Manager's concern with productivity, for example:
'I'm worried about:
- the General Manager's PA interrupting us over a supplier's telephone call;
- the General Manager's response to this interruption;
- the supervisor speaking only in the absence of the General Manager'.

Having created a long list of worries or issues, it is sensible to try to create some sort of structure among them. They are likely to be related in some ways, so a simple method is to cluster them around similar themes.

These diagrams in various forms are called mind maps, spidergrams, or cause and effect diagrams. This layout can often stimulate further thoughts and ideas.

This technique is applied to the case study in Exhibit 2.5, which shows the issues relating to the purpose of improving productivity at ICC.

It shows the purpose (improve productivity) at the centre of the diagram. Around it are shown the issues that have been cited before, which have been grouped according to theme. Issues can appear in more than one place if that seems appropriate; for example, in the diagram, machine downtime appears twice (on the equipment theme, and on the systems theme as a contributory cause of operative waiting time).

In practice, the best way of going about this is first to create an unstructured list of issues and then to map them on to the cause and effect diagram as shown. Writing the ideas on the diagram will help to create more ideas about what others might be appropriate.

Exhibit 2.5 Issues shown on a cause and effect diagram

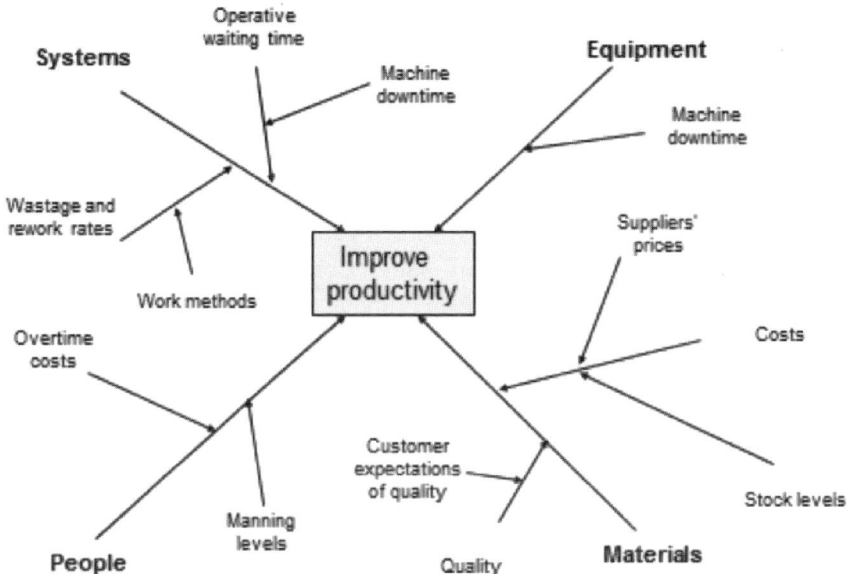

The Exhibit does not show issues outside the General Manager's presenting concern; these could be the subject of a separate diagram and will be a function of deciding where to start and your freedom so to do (see below).

As a practical tip, if a consultant team is involved, then it is useful to do this work as a 'case conference', sharing perceptions, understanding and experience.

Remember that issue analysis is not conclusive; a number of these issues identified will be speculative at best and will need further information before they can be validated. So issue analysis can be a useful pointer to a requirement for further data.

LEVELS OF INTERVENTION

The issues identified in the ICC case study are of different scale; for example:
- 'Increase the reliability of the packaging machine on the C production line';
- 'Replace the General Manager as he is incompetent'.

The latter would require a more profound intervention than the former; indeed, it might not be an option.

The notion of 'levels of intervention' enables you to decide the appropriate starting point for a consultancy project. They can be defined as:

1. *Purposes:* The aims that the client has in mind when inviting consultancy help.
2. *Problems:* The problem areas that must be addressed if the purposes are to be achieved.
3. *Solutions:* What the solutions should be.
4. *Implementation:* The plans and activities for resolving the problem by introducing the chosen solutions.

After the visit the General Manager (GM) of ICC might call up John Smith saying, 'As you can see, our main problem is the C production line. We obviously need to refurbish the equipment, and we'd like you to oversee the project.' A level 4 intervention would be for John Smith to implement the GM's plans and support the refurbishment.

At a level 3 intervention, John Smith would accept the GM's diagnosis of the problem, but might question the solution. He might look for other ways of improving productivity on the 'C' production line – for example, by improved methods, materials flow or planning.

If John Smith intervened at level 2, he might identify other issues that could contribute to high production costs, besides those of the 'C' production line. During his visit, he might note:
- operatives idle while the packaging machine was being fixed;
- large piles of rejects;
- high overtime costs;
- high supplier prices;
- unchanged specifications.

He would need to check whether these are important contributory factors to high production costs; there may be other issues too, which need consideration.

Finally, if John Smith made a level 1 intervention, he would query the General Manager's initial statement of purpose. Is it true that the production costs of his competitors are less? Does the financial structure of the cutlery business mean that ICC can match their competitors? Would it be worthwhile? Indeed, there appears to be plenty that is wrong; is this a failure of the General Manager himself? Is management failing? It would be interesting to know how long the General Manager has been in post. If recently appointed, we can understand why he wants expert help to improve productivity; if he has been in post for 10 years, why now? These are all questions John Smith might ask at this level.

Although we have defined four levels, they are on a continuum. For example, the more precisely a problem becomes defined and understood, the closer you get to a solution.

Each level proceeds on the basis of assumptions about the earlier level; for example, if your level of intervention is about formulating solutions, then this will be predicated on assumptions about the nature of the problems that have to be addressed. Similarly, the definition of problems will follow assumptions about purposes – what is to be achieved in the first place.

Going back to the ICC case study example, having identified the levels of intervention John Smith could make, you can see that the intervention at level 4 cited first is based on assumptions about the preceding levels, namely that:
- ICC's competitors have a cost advantage and ICC must reduce production costs in order to compete; (level 1).
- Improving performance on the C production line will have a worthwhile impact on productivity; (level 2).
- Refurbishing the machinery will improve productivity on the C production line; (level 3).
- So implementing the GM's refurbishment plans will make ICC more competitive; (level 4).

There is a clear correlation between this model of levels of intervention and the model of progressive definition shown in Exhibit 2.4.

CHOOSING WHERE TO START

A simple rule is 'start at the point of uncertainty' and the levels of intervention model is a helpful way of thinking about this. Part of your expertise should be to judge at which level of intervention it is necessary to start and to guide your clients accordingly.

At the start of any involvement with a client (i.e. before a project has been defined) you must therefore ask the question: 'Can I take as read any assumptions about the levels above that at which I am operating, on which my work is predicated? Or is there a piece of work that needs to be done to check these out before I engage in the main piece of work?'

Thinking at a degree of freedom more than that of the client means questioning the assumptions on which a client's construction of any problem is based. For example, a large company decided to make its IT department perform better by insisting that it dealt with all internal 'customers' on a commercial basis. Other departments would then be free to use other sources of IT services if they could be provided more cheaply.

The manager of the IT department had considerable misgivings about this. Although there would be short-term cost savings, she believed that in the long term the quality of IT systems and support would fall. She decided to proceed with implementing this proposal, however, and discussed how it might be best accomplished with an outside consultant.

The consultant had at this point to choose at what level to intervene. A level 4 intervention would have meant setting up the IT department so that it could function effectively on a commercial basis. With a level 3 intervention (a degree of freedom greater than the client was thinking) the consultant would have looked at other ways in which the IT department could improve its service to other parts of the organisation.

In the event, on questioning from the consultant, the manager disclosed her misgivings about this solution. Further probing revealed that the problem was really that internal departments resented the way that IT was costed into their budgets as an overhead, rather than for services received. This meant that alternative solutions – changing the costing system – became more appropriate, and this was the one eventually adopted.

Dealing with clients on these matters has to be handled sensitively to avoid appearing to be extending the scope of an assignment needlessly. On the domestic front, we do not welcome our plumber's help on matters other than plumbing – his advice on our financial affairs, for example, would be intrusive. Similarly, a client may become irritated with a training consultant who tries needlessly to develop a training assignment into matters of corporate strategy. Where a problem is clearly and satisfactorily defined, intervening at level 3, to define solutions, is entirely proper.

Of course, you may well have biases or preferences about where you start on a project. This will be strongly influenced by the type of consultancy in which you specialise. For example:
- A strategy consultant may always start by questioning the purposes of a client (level 1);
- A management consultant may focus on identifying problems (level 2) and recommending how they might be resolved (level 3);
- A technical consultant will help with defining solutions (level 3) and how they might be implemented (level 4).

It is important to recognise these biases because you may be required to work at different levels. For example, an IT consultant may need to clarify problems in order to do the job. Similarly, a strategy consultant may need to follow a project through to detailed implementation. Under these circumstances, the project may be broken into separate phases, each dealing with the question at different levels of intervention.

PHASING

If you start a project with a level 4 intervention, then you can predict with a fair degree of confidence how the project will develop.

By contrast, with a level 1 intervention it is more difficult to predict what will happen, as work at subsequent levels will depend on the findings of those preceding. Under these circumstances an iterative approach is appropriate, which breaks the consultancy project down into phases, as shown in Exhibit 2.6.

Exhibit 2.6 Successive levels of intervention should be treated as different phases of a project

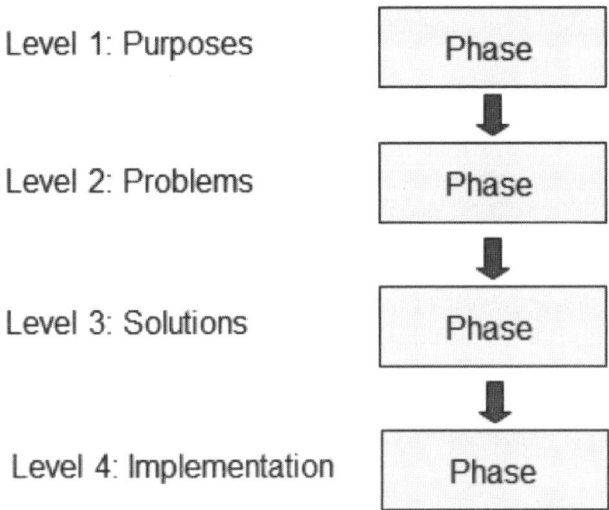

The work at each level is best dealt with as a separate phase in a project. This implies that in carrying a project through from clarifying purposes to implementing solutions, there should be at least four phases. If you start at level 3, however, you could manage with just two phases. Each phase, of course, could itself be a project with several stages involved.

The example of ICC can be used to illustrate phasing, as follows:

The GM telephones John Smith to say that he's concerned about the competitiveness of ICC, and he believes that production costs need to be reduced. John Smith visits the factory; his visit is reported in the account given earlier in this chapter. Based on his appraisal, John Smith accepts the GM's view of the purposes, and decides to start with a level 2 intervention, identifying the problems which lead to high production costs.

At the end of this phase, John Smith might report to the GM with his appraisal of the problems that must be addressed if ICC's production costs are to be reduced. The GM might then ask, 'What should we do to address these problems?'

This is a level 3 intervention, which therefore forms the next phase of the project. When this is complete, John Smith would report to the GM with recommendations on how problems can be mitigated or solved.

Finally, the GM might ask John Smith to implement his recommendations (a level 4 intervention).

Of course, you may not be able to start at the level you ideally would like, perhaps because of your level of entry into the client organisation, or because of your client's expectations of you. In such a case it may be best to start at a lower level of intervention and seek to understand the situation better as well as providing help to the client. With a better understanding – and a closer relationship with the client – it may then be possible to present your views in a way that the client accepts.

THE PROBLEM SOLVING APPROACH

We have seen that:
1. The consultant's first task is to define the questions that need to be answered to resolve the client's predicament.
2. The idea of 'levels of intervention' can direct attention to the type of questions to be asked.

We have also noted that it is helpful to have a process that will enable the questions to be addressed, and this is set out below.

OUTLINE OF THE APPROACH

We noted earlier that consultants and clients arrive at situations with preconceptions and these, together with experience and expertise, may provide some promising routes for following up solutions. The problem solving method is one adapted from a method familiar to scientists: that of developing hypotheses, which are then tested through the collection of suitable data.

In what follows, I shall define an *assumption* as valid: it does not need to be checked out and can be prefaced with the word 'certainly'. In contrast, I shall define a *hypothesis* as a supposition that is only conjectural, i.e. it needs to be checked out before we can accept it. A hypothesis is a contention; some people find it helpful to preface it, like a debating topic, with the words, 'This house believes...', or even more simply with the words 'perhaps' or 'maybe'. An assumption can be taken as read, but a hypothesis needs data collection to verify it. For example, take the statement, 'It is raining'; if it is an assumption, you will take it to be true and take an umbrella if you go out. If it is a hypothesis ('Perhaps it is raining') this implies that you are not sure whether it is indeed raining, and may wish to check before taking your umbrella.

The way in which preconceptions can be accommodated is by regarding them as hypothetical; similarly, all the ideas you have at the start of a project can provide fuel for hypotheses.

Hypotheses provide a guide to data collection, which is directed towards checking them out. The problem solving approach based on hypotheses is shown in Exhibit 2.7.

The approach starts with hypotheses, which are generated from experience, evidence and by creative thinking. This creative stage is followed by an evaluative stage in which you select which hypotheses to investigate. Data collection is directed at verifying these selected hypotheses; during data collection you may also come up with further hypotheses. Finally, you arrive at conclusions. A conclusion can be thought of as a proven hypothesis; conversely a hypothesis can be thought of as a provisional conclusion.

Exhibit 2.7 The problem solving approach

```
┌─────────────────────────────────────────┐
│ Use creative thinking to generate hypotheses │◄──────┐
└──────────────────┬──────────────────────┘       │
                   ▼                               │
┌─────────────────────────────────────────┐       │
│      Select which to investigate         │       │
└──────────────────┬──────────────────────┘       │
                   ▼                               │
┌─────────────────────────────────────────┐   ┌───────────────────────┐
│  Identify the data you need to verify these │   │  Form new hypotheses   │
└──────────────────┬──────────────────────┘   │  in the light of this data │
                   ▼                           └───────────▲───────────┘
┌─────────────────────────────────────────┐               │
│             Collect the data             │               │
└──────────────────┬──────────────────────┘               │
                   ▼                                       │
┌─────────────────────────────────────────┐               │
│             Analyse the data             │───────────────┘
└──────────────────┬──────────────────────┘
                   ▼
┌─────────────────────────────────────────┐
│           Arrive at conclusions          │
└─────────────────────────────────────────┘
```

CREATIVE THINKING IN CONSULTANCY

Creative thinking was mentioned in the previous section as a method of creating hypotheses.

If there is a characteristic that distinguishes excellent consultants from the merely good, it is that of creativity. One consultant defines creativity as, 'that which is obvious only in retrospect'. My own experience endorses this when working with a colleague or client whose insight provides the key to finding the way forward in resolving a problem. Or, in my own work, having struggled with defining a way forward, stumbling on the key and reflecting, 'Why on earth didn't I think of that before – it seems so obvious (now!)'

People are naturally creative but are often educated out of it. One has only to look at a group of children playing anywhere in the world to realise that creativity is an innate human characteristic. As an adult, to become more creative you must reduce the barriers to creativity. Roger von Oech in his book *A whack on the side of the head* (Business Plus Imports, 2008) identifies ten barriers to creative thinking. They are shown below:

The right answer	That's not logical
Follow the rules	Be practical
Avoid ambiguity	To err is wrong
Play is frivolous	That is not my area
Don't be foolish	I am not creative

All these rules are appropriate at some time or another. For example, we may not be very enthusiastic to hear a surgeon describe the operation they are about to carry out on us as outside their specialisation, or that they might be experimenting with a new technique that has a high risk of failure compared with other ones that he might use. Similarly, we do not want our bankers to be using our money in risky and creative ways if it means that we might lose it. Creativity, therefore, has to be applied appropriately. There is a time to be creative, using divergent thinking; there is a time to be analytical, evaluating the ideas created.

Typically, though, people working in groups mix creative and evaluative thinking. Someone will come up with an idea, which will then be evaluated by the whole group. (Sometimes evaluation consists in completely overlooking it!) The process that is being used is that of creating an idea and then evaluating it, repeating the process as required.

This process of cycling between creative thinking and then evaluative thinking ('mixed thinking') inhibits creativity. Many of the 'barriers to creativity' quoted above are quite appropriate when engaged in evaluative thinking. When engaging in mixed thinking, sometimes the barriers will be in place, some of the time they will be suspended. The problem for a participant in a problem solving meeting is discerning whether they are in place or suspended; the safe bet is to assume that they are in place. What therefore happens is that evaluative thinking takes over and few ideas are created.

A useful method of dealing with this difficulty is to separate the idea creation process from that of evaluation, into two explicit stages. First you generate lots of ideas, and then only after you have finished this stage do you pick out the ones that merit further investigation.

This latter process of separated thinking is used in brainstorming techniques. In brainstorming there is a creative period, where the aim is to create a large quantity of ideas irrespective of quality, because quality implies evaluation. Evaluation is suspended until a later analytical period.

Techniques for creating ideas

The classic approach to brainstorming suggests various techniques for generating ideas. One such is 'freewheeling' – just noting ideas as they pop into your head. Another is (when working in a group) to let an idea suggested by one person stimulate others.

Both these techniques, however, start with some notion of the idea under consideration and move on from there. An alternative technique is to start from somewhere completely different and see whether that gives you new insights. For instance, you could start with a completely random set of words, and see how they might relate to the problem under consideration. (Sometimes this is known as 'random entry technique'.) Take a few of the words that have been used in the last few pages:

Working	Random
Motion	Completely
Alternatives	Struggled

Consider the problem quoted above of improving performance at International Cutlery Company. You would then try to see if any of the words above might provide an insight that you previously had not considered. What relationship might there be, for example, between 'struggled' and 'improving performance?' Setting a group exercise where operations are challenged to find ways of improving performance might be an idea linking the two.

Another technique is to use metaphor or analogy; for example, what insights can we get if this problem is thought of as a water distribution system? A piece of music? A meal? And there are other techniques, covered in many books.

The first step in the technique is to develop hypotheses; these should vary according to the level of intervention. Exhibit 2.8 shows the assumptions and hypotheses for each level.

Exhibit 2.8 Assumptions and hypotheses at each level of intervention

	Assumptions ('certainly')	*Hypotheses ('perhaps')*
1	There is a predicament that merits attention	What purposes should we therefore consider?
2	The purposes to be achieved	What problems stand in the way of achieving this purpose?
3	The problems that must be addressed	How might they be resolved?
4	The solutions that must be put in place	How might they best be implemented?

Points to note are:
- Hypotheses at a given level of intervention are related to the outputs for that level.
- The hypotheses for one level are assumptions for the next, hence each level should be dealt with as a separate phase.

- If your thinking is to be 'one degree of freedom more than that of the client', then what you do is to treat the client's assumptions as hypotheses.

To illustrate these processes we will again refer to the International Cutlery Company case study set out above.

Assume that at the end of his visit, John Smith, the consultant, has decided to accept the GM's declared purpose of improving productivity so there is no need for intervention at level 1. This purpose therefore is the assumption underlying level 2, and so John Smith would start at this level by using creative thinking to develop hypotheses about the problems that relate to low productivity. He would derive these hypotheses from his observations during his visit, his knowledge and previous experience and his imagination.

John Smith may, of course, have created ideas that are not hypotheses about problems, but relate to other levels of intervention; for example, 'The GM is useless and should be fired'. This is a hypothesis about a solution; it is appropriate for level 3, but not for level 2 at which John Smith is currently working. He can use it, though, to identify further problems by asking, 'To what problem would this solution relate?' This solution is about 'the quality of management', so he could add 'quality of management' as a further problem he might investigate.

Practical hints in defining hypotheses

Some practical tips in carrying out this process:

- If you are working in a group in developing ideas, it is common to use a flip chart to record them. When they are coming thick and fast, it is difficult for whoever is doing the writing to get down all the detail. In such circumstances, it is usual practice to abbreviate or to abstract the ideas. This is a dangerous practice. By abstraction or abbreviation, much of the richness of the ideas is lost and where they are expressed imprecisely, it becomes very difficult to verify them (as we shall see when we come to looking at data collection).
- A better method is for members of the group to start writing all their ideas on 'post-its' with a separate one for each, and then stick them on the wall. Members of the group then look at them and do a second round. This process can continue and morph into the group's discussion more commonly associated with brainstorming.
- Sometimes the reverse is the case. When recording ideas during a creative session, those responsible for writing them down often behave as if ink was highly expensive! So write down all the ideas and then evaluate them; if the scribe acts as editor, it means that the evaluation is happening prematurely. Don't worry if you have some ideas that appear totally irrelevant during the initial trawl for them; they can be edited out later.

SELECTING HYPOTHESES

Following up every hypothesis is not practical or necessary, so some process of hypothesis selection is required. This is where you have to exercise your judgement, based on your expertise.

The stages involved in selecting which hypotheses are to be pursued are as follows:
1. Disregard those hypotheses that are not relevant to the issues being studied. If the process of hypothesis creation has been dealt with properly, lots of ideas will have been recorded that have very little relevance to the scope of the project. By a process of inspection, disregard those that seem completely irrelevant. If in doubt, leave the ideas in.
2. Assess the remainder according to their relevance and probability. For example at ICC, the motivation of sales staff may be an issue, but it does not appear immediately relevant to the purpose of increasing productivity. John Smith may also have hypothesised that, 'Competing manufacturers are engaged in sabotage'; this is improbable, so again it is one that would not be pursued as a matter of priority.
3. Hypotheses should be then classified into three categories:
   A: Those which must be investigated because they are of central importance:
   C: Those which could be investigated, but only if there was time.

The missing category, B, is for those that you are unsure whether to put into category A or C.

After this process, you should have a shortlist of hypotheses that you are going to follow up through the process of data collection. It is a good idea at this point to take stock of your list of hypotheses; do they seem sufficient to you?

This is a sort of reality test; if you feel that having gone through this process you would still want to explore some items outside those hypotheses, it usually means that there are hypotheses that you have not yet articulated. If you feel unhappy, therefore, think carefully through what you have so far done. Is there anything missing from the logic? If so, what is it?

DATA COLLECTION

The problem solving method is about taking a structured approach to understanding a client's predicament. We saw, however, that there are some areas where you can confidently assume the correctness of your views while in others they should be regarded as hypothetical or speculative.

Exhibit 2.7 showed the stages involved. Data collection is shown as a means by which you can test hypotheses, proving them to be true or false or at least shedding a little light on them. But we should never lose sight of the fact that consultancy projects are a means to an end, that end being to the benefit of the client. So the Exhibit can be redrawn as an input-output model, as shown in Exhibit 2.9. The scope of the consultancy project will determine the nature of the deliverables to the client. Hypotheses can be regarded as provisional conclusions, while conclusions can be regarded as proven hypotheses. The data that is collected will be a function of the data specification. So there is a symmetry about inputs and outputs as well as the sequence shown in Exhibit 2.7. Data collection is key to this process.

Exhibit 2.9 The problem solving approach as an input/output model

Input	Output	
Client's predicament	Benefits for client	Ends for the client
Scope of consultancy project	Deliverables to client	Means embodied in the consultancy project
Hypotheses	Conclusions	
Data specification	→ Data collection	

There are two essential considerations in data collection: defining what data is required and using an appropriate method to gather it.

DEFINING WHAT DATA IS REQUIRED

Data collection is a time consuming element in any consultancy project and also one of the most expensive. It is essential that you are clear about what data you are aiming to collect and why you are doing so. It is very easy for the intellectually curious to go along some cul-de-sacs and expensively collect data that has little relevance to the questions in hand. The process of data collection should therefore be directed to verifying the hypotheses that you have selected.

On this basis, you could produce a specification of what data is required, and then go out and collect it. In practice, consultancy requires more. One feature of first engaging with a new client or project is the process of familiarisation. The consultant has to get to know the client – the people, the culture, the business processes and structure – and the client has to learn how to accommodate the consultant and the project being undertaken. Each is progressing along a learning curve about the other, and it is unusual for familiarisation to be embodied in a formal process of data collection.

Exhibit 2.10 Data collection evolves with the project

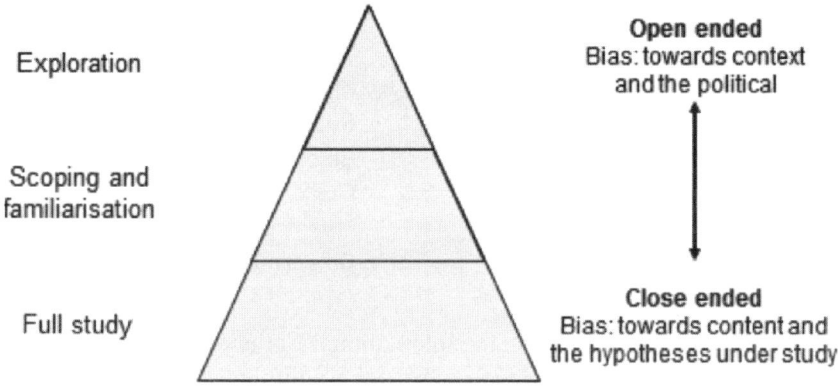

Exhibit 2.10 shows how the scope of a project evolves and the nature of data collection that goes along with it.

Early in the project, you need to develop a feel for the political environment in the client. Data collection therefore is open-ended, and you will be concerned with opinions as much as facts. Next, you will generate and revise hypotheses during this scoping and familiarisation phase (it is worth noting that you may wish to revise your hypotheses as a result of data collection). Once you have established your shortlist of hypotheses, then your data collection can become more focused on the data you need to check out your selected hypotheses.

Data collection can be of two broad kinds: 1. Open ended, where you cannot be precise about what it is you need to know; 2. Close ended, where you know exactly what you need to find out.

As shown in Exhibit 2.10, open ended data collection is more appropriate during the early stages of a project.

Open ended data specification

Here it is useful to create an exploratory agenda. Typically, it will consist of areas of interest or enquiry that you want to explore, with perhaps subsidiary topics that you want specifically to look at.

The specification can be generated simply from the sort of cause and effect analysis shown in Exhibit 2.5. The main legs of the diagram could provide the areas of enquiry, which the branches from them could point towards the topics that you want information on. So the data specification could appear as in Exhibit 2.11 below.

Exhibit 2.11 Open ended data specification

	Area of enquiry		Topic
1.	Systems	1.1	Operative waiting time
		1.2	Machine downtime
		1.3	Wastage and rework rates
		1.4	Method
2.	Equipment	2.1	Machine downtime
3.	Materials	3.1	Supplies prices
		3.2	Stock levels
		3.3	Customer expectations of quality
4.	People	4.1	Manning levels
		4.2	Downtime costs

In this example, taken from the International Cutlery Company example, each of the topics relates to an issue that John Smith may want to explore in more detail.

What often happens is that information gathered in the early exploratory stages prompts new ideas of what data is important to collect and the data specification is modified accordingly.

Close ended data specification

When engaged in close-ended data collection, you can specify more precisely:
- what data you need;
- what form it might take – e.g. what units is it measured in?
- where you might find it.

Specifying precisely what data you need becomes particularly important when working in teams of consultants; each member of the team must be clear what data they have to collect. For example, a multi-country study would be of little use if the information from each country was not compatible, because different consultants had interpreted what was required in different ways.

To illustrate the process of data specification, we will again consider the ICC case study, but at a level 3 intervention – one at which the issues have been confirmed and the work now consists of identifying how best they might be addressed.

Suppose that the issue John Smith is to investigate is that of overtime costs, and that he has selected hypotheses for the problems underlying this issue as follows:
- There is too much work for the labour force;
- People are not working hard enough;
- People are not sufficiently skilled;
- Work is poorly planned;
- Overtime pay rates are high.

Practice differs in consultancies in how they set out a data specification. Some consultancies identify what is called a 'research question related to each hypothesis'. This is a question, which if answered, would help you to judge whether the hypothesis is true.

The perfect question would simply be an inversion of the hypothesis: thus in the list of hypotheses quoted above, the hypothesis 'too much work for the labour force' would invite the research question 'Is there too much work for the labour force?' Indeed, some consultancies do not distinguish between hypotheses and research questions – confusingly, they call them all 'questions'. I prefer the split into hypotheses and research questions as a research question can be phrased to illuminate one part of a hypothesis.

Research questions are particularly helpful if the hypothesis is expressed very generally and has to be focused before any work can be done in investigating whether it is true. This depends on the degree of abstraction of an idea. An example of increasing degrees of abstraction is as follows:
- Spot is a small, playful and furry thing.
- Spot is a puppy.
- A puppy is a pet.
- A pet is an animal.

'Spot' is a specific, concrete idea; 'animal' is far more general and abstract. A hypothesis about Spot will be easier to verify than one about animals in general.

The 'research question' technique can therefore be used to help to reduce the degree of abstraction of a hypothesis. In the ICC case study, for example, you might come up with the hypothesis 'Quality is poor'. This is abstract and difficult to verify, but could be made more concrete through research questions such as:
- Are wastage rates above the industry average?
- Do customers return goods as being of inadequate quality?
- Are quality standards set higher than those of competitors?

Once the key question has been phrased, a data specification can be prepared. As noted above, a data specification defines:

- what data is required;
- what format it might be in;
- where it might be found.

The data specification also shows checks: where there is a particularly crucial piece of data that is required, you may wish to have more than one source of it. Exhibit 2.12 shows a completed data specification for collecting information about International Cutlery Company's overtime costs and how they compare with those elsewhere.

Exhibit 2.12 Close ended data specification

Data	Format	Sources	Checks
Current pay in ICC for overtime	Hourly rates, basis of variation	Personnel department	Do these reconcile?
Current distribution of overtime earnings	By grade, dept., job category	Personnel department	
Any local or industry agreements	Terms of agreement	Personnel department	
What local companies are comparable?	List of likely competitors for labour	Local Chamber of Commerce	ICC Personnel Dept.
What overtime rates are paid in those companies?	Same format as ICC	Company personnel department	Recruitment agencies

Compromise is often necessary

Data is expensive to collect, in terms of time, and thus in money. Having determined what data is necessary and sufficient, you may need to reduce this still further due to shortage of time or other limiting factors. The need for compromise is raised here, because hard data is sometimes difficult or impossible to collect. For example, it may be desirable to know the market prices of each supplier of widgets across the world, but official statistics may not cover this, and the manufacturers themselves could be reluctant to provide them to you. Alternatively you could be subject to disinformation. A compromise may be made by substituting qualitative for quantitative data, and opinion or consensus in the absence of objective data.

The latter is particularly necessary with soft data – that relating, for example, to views and opinions. Soft data is important when dealing with recommendations or matters of implementation, when recognition of the political climate, and the culture and values of an organisation, may be essential in achieving acceptance. The more senior your client, the more likely they are to be concerned about soft issues and data, such as those concerning competitiveness, communication and morale.

CHOOSING A METHOD OF DATA COLLECTION

There are four generic methods of collecting data:
- Face to face from other people;
- Remotely from other people, by using questionnaires or similar documents;
- Looking at documents and records;
- Direct observation.

Each has its pros and cons, which are summarised in Exhibit 2.13.

Exhibit 2.13 Pros and cons of different methods of data collection

Method of data collection	Pros	Cons
Interviews one to one	Personal contact with the interviewee Unstructured – you can follow up points of interest The interviewee has made a clear contribution Enables you to judge what sort of person the interviewee is	Time consuming Difficult to decide who to see Time consuming to analyse
Interviews one with a group	You can meet more people The project has a higher profile	Hard work – probably needs two people Less opportunity for individuals to contribute People may be inhibited from contributing
Questionnaires	You can collect a large number of views A well designed questionnaire should be easy to analyse The respondent can fill in as and when they want Is not time consuming for client staff	Close-ended; you get answers only to the questions you ask Must be self-explanatory Respondents may have reservations about committing their views to writing No sense of strength of feeling or relevance (although you can put in scales to test this) Low response rates
Document Inspection	Good chance of getting unexpected data You can go at your own rate	Limited availability of documentation Time consuming for consultant Can be difficult to find the data wanted
Observation	First-hand information Good chance of picking up something unexpected	Observation can affect the system being observed Time consuming Difficult to analyse

But quite apart from their intrinsic merits, when you have to choose a method for collecting the data you need, there are four other criteria to be met:

- Is it sufficiently open-ended? Will it collect the data required on the hypotheses being explored? It is important that wrong assumptions are not built in (e.g. as in the question 'When did you stop beating your wife?')
- Will it collect the 'soft data' required? This relates to people's opinions. These will be particularly important in considering the acceptability (or otherwise) of recommendations, for example. Hard data by itself leads to idealistic solutions; soft data provides information on how to make them workable and acceptable.
- What will its impact be? Remember that data collection is an intervention into an organisation. This, if poorly handled, can have dysfunctional effects. On the other hand, the data collection method can be used to suggest processes of desirable change, or to give the project a suitable profile in the organisation.
- Is it economical and effective?

Finally, remember that as data collection is itself an intervention into the client's organisation, it is not possible for you to carry it out without in some way affecting the views of the client's staff about you, your practice and the project you are undertaking. A well-constructed and executed data collection programme can enhance your credibility, yield high quality solutions and help to ensure more ready acceptance of your recommendations.

Interviewing skills

Much of the data will be collected using interviews. Your interview plan should reflect the type of data that you require to answer the key questions related to your hypotheses. Bear in mind that you could have objectives for the meeting other than data collection, such as:
- building relationships with the interviewee;
- giving information;
- canvassing support for a particular view or opinion;
- problem solving;
- decision making.

Remember to leave sufficient time in an interview schedule for data analysis as well as collection; for example, to write up or consolidate interview notes and to relate the data to your hypotheses. Interviewing requires sustained concentration and is tiring, so do not try to pack in too many interviews in a short time. A good rule of thumb is to allocate twice as much time to an interview programme as the time you expect to spend face to face with interviewees.

Try to structure data collection in a logical order so that key questions are answered first, and so that you avoid carrying out data collection which subsequently proves needless. Aim to get the data with the greatest 'leverage' first. For example, if the support of a Managing Director is crucial to the acceptance of your proposals, you need to find out if they have any strong dislikes or preferences fairly quickly, and this could condition which hypotheses you select to pursue.

DATA ANALYSIS AND CONCLUSIONS

The data collection process accumulates facts, which then have to be processed to produce conclusions. Ideally, what should have happened is that the case for or against each hypothesis should have been made. A proven hypothesis is a conclusion, and so the conclusions from a full study would be a list of the hypotheses that had been proven.

Consultancy is more expedient than science and so, sadly, rarely as rigorous as this. The whole process is a little more messy. Nonetheless, it is essential that your conclusions stand up to examination, like the layers of skin in an onion. Peeling away the top layer shows another layer as fine as the first; peeling the second layer away reveals a third, and so on. So too should it be with a consultant's thinking. For example, it is said of a former chief executive of an international firm that if you went to him with a proposal, he would take one part of your case, and ask, 'Why?' of it. He would then take an aspect of your answer, and ask 'Why?' of that. He would then ask 'Why?' of an aspect of your next answer. If you could answer these three layers of questions satisfactorily, he would accept that you had thought through your case.

Three layers of thinking can be thought of in data analysis:
1. *Data* – the facts you have collected.
2. *Findings* – an evaluation of these facts. (This usually relies on unspecified data, such as a standard or normal practice.)
3. *Conclusions* – the diagnosis drawn from the evaluation.

The interventions that are required to address the areas of concern can then be specified according to the conclusions. Interventions are of varying kinds; frequently they consist of recommendations for the client's action, but they might also be action by the consultant, such as:
- training client staff;
- conducting a further project;
- taking an executive role;
- supporting the work of an individual or group.

For example:
It is raining (a piece of data).
The weather is bad (finding). (This is evaluative because the rain

may not be bad for a farmer whose crops need rain; the unspecified piece of data is that we want the weather to be fine.)
We cannot go for a picnic (conclusion).
We should eat lunch indoors (recommendation).

Exhibit 2.14 From data to recommendations

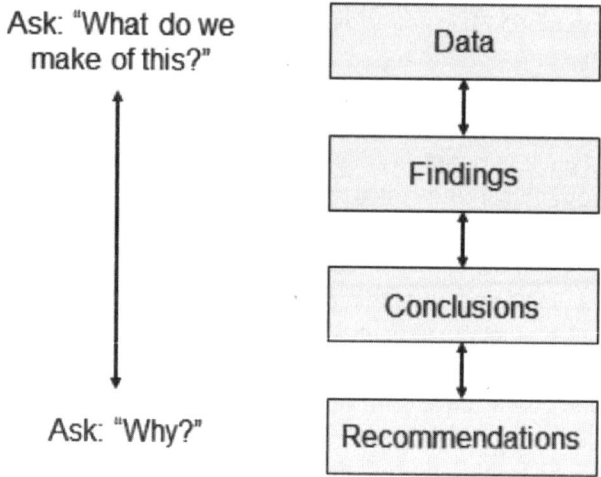

Exhibit 2.14 shows the relationship:
1. Data lead to findings.
2. Findings draw you to conclusions.
3. The specification of the intervention(s) is based on conclusions.

Each step leads to the next by asking 'What do we make of this, in respect of the topics we are examining?' Also, the logic can be tested in reverse by asking, 'Why – what leads us to this view?'

Of course, in practice the process of splitting data, findings and conclusions under the headings shown can be a messy process. You can have difficulty sorting out what is a piece of data, a finding or a conclusion. A practical technique for dealing with this ambiguity is:
- Divide a large piece of newsprint/flip chart paper into three columns, headed 'Data', 'Findings', 'Conclusions'.
- Write your data, findings and conclusions on 'Post It' or similar type labels.
- Stick them under the appropriate headings and inspect to see whether they are correctly allocated.

Use of these labels means that you can move a comment from one heading to another. A major criterion to use is that they all fit together.

Once you are happy you have allocated your labels correctly, you should ask the following questions of your analysis:
- Does the data lead logically to the findings and the findings to the conclusions? In particular, are there any alternative interpretations that could be made at any stage?
- Are there key findings that have not been substantiated, which could be used to corroborate the conclusions?
- Do the findings rest crucially on a narrow range of data? What would be the result if this data were inaccurate, and how inaccurate would it have to be before you changed your conclusions? How likely is it to be inaccurate? Thus the links between the various stages are tested.

There remains the final and most important test, which is to refer back to the project objectives:
- Will the interventions specified satisfactorily address the areas of concern put to us? Have we met our commitments to producing outputs? Will our conclusions form a sufficient basis to move the project ahead?

The project objectives should be held in mind throughout the project. It is easy to stray away from the original objectives and specify interventions which, although totally logical and valid, fail to meet the client's original concerns. Remember to re-read your original proposal regularly during the project.

3

OPERATING A CONSULTANCY PROJECT

A former colleague once explained his view of consultancy thus: 'We are in the business of selling people their dreams,' he said. 'Consultants are the dream merchants of business.' This may be the case, but dreams turn into nightmares when consultants promise the unattainable to a client. At the best they will have a damaged reputation; in these increasingly litigious times, they may end up being sued.

All that a client buys on purchasing an assignment is a promise; unlike for example a car salesman, a consultant cannot point to the product and say, 'This is what you're going to get.'

What you actually get depends on the skills of the consultants delivering the project. In this chapter we consider first the way in which consultancy projects are structured and the skills applying to each phase. Second, we review the demands that consultancy projects make in respect of project management.

THE STRUCTURE OF A CONSULTANCY PROJECT

Irrespective of the level of intervention or the number of phases in a consultancy project, you will find that this structure of a project will be similar. The structure of a consultancy project can be broken down into the major stages as shown in Exhibit 3.1.

Exhibit 3.1 The structure of a consultancy project

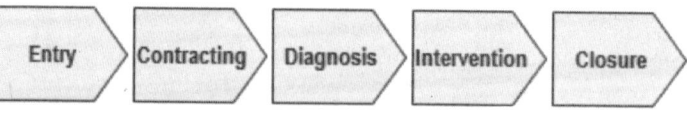

ENTRY

Your first contact with a client may be in selling an assignment or starting an assignment that has already been sold. In either case, careful preparation is required and you should aim to make a favourable impact: there is no second chance to make a first impression.

Early in any project it is important to allow time for familiarisation. This will be necessary not only for practical matters (such as who's who, office layout) but also for understanding the informal rules and climate of the organisation. This I call a 'wallow'; it is unstructured data collection, which allows you to soak up the atmosphere and culture of an organisation, to learn its 'language' and the myriad of other features that characterise it.

The skills of entry will be covered in Chapter 7 on selling: when consultants meet new clients, they are 'selling' themselves in this role. No further remarks on this are given here.

CONTRACTING

Contracting is about having shared expectations between client and consultant as to what is involved in the project.

Selling consultancy is very much a process of product design as well as persuading a client to purchase your services. It is therefore essential to be clear what exactly you are selling, and the specification can be best encompassed in terms of reference, dealt with in detail in the sections below.

As soon as contact is made there will be expectations created and commitments made on both sides. These are in addition to the formal agreement set out in the terms of reference.

Expectations relate not only to meeting commitments in the terms of reference, but also in how you carry out the project, e.g. the apparent priority you attach to the work you are doing for the client. You will also have expectations of the client; these will be reflected largely in the commitment the client shows towards the project.

The sponsor – the member of the client's staff commissioning the project – will, presumably, be committed to it, but you have to consider the commitment of others. Will the project require the co-operation of more senior or more junior staff and, if so, are they committed to the project? Beware of sponsors who are not committed to the project or (at the opposite extreme) who are carrying it out as a personal crusade.

Contracting also covers the practicalities at the start of a project:
- Where will you be working and with what facilities?
- What is the project plan (if this has not been included in the terms of reference)?

- What support will you receive from the client and what form will this take?
- Who will you be dealing with among client staff?
- What have client staff been told about the project – what are their expectations?

DIAGNOSIS

Diagnosis consists of data collection, its analysis and then diagnosis.

Paradoxically, you need to consider analysis before deciding what data you need to gather; you have to know what you are going to do with it when you have it. Data gathering is time consuming and you need to make sure you confine yourself to gathering only that which is necessary and sufficient for your purposes. (See Chapter 2.)

The diagnosis should be drawn from the data collected and consists of conclusions about the nature of the problems being addressed and how they might be resolved. Conclusions answer the question, 'What is the relevance of this data to the areas of concern we are examining?'

Diagnosis comprises much of the work on a project and so 'managing consulting projects' is covered under this heading below.

INTERVENTION

As a result of the diagnosis, you can then specify the intervention that needs to be made.

Because consultants rarely have executive authority within their clients, most often the intervention specified will be in the form of recommendations to be adopted by the client. Whether or not recommendations are accepted is, at least in part, dependent on the influence of the consultant; this topic is discussed later in this chapter.

CLOSURE

Closure marks the completion of a project. When you leave the client, they should have an ongoing capability to maintain the changes and improvements you have introduced as a result of your work. *Transfer* is the process of so doing, and is discussed further at the end of the chapter.

It is also important to carry out some sort of *evaluation* of the assignment once it has been completed. This is important not only for quality assurance purposes, but also to ensure that the consultancy practice gets value from the

experience of the consultancy team who have carried out the job, for example by capturing:
- the experience of having carried out this work;
- any new operating techniques that have been developed during the project;
- the experience and credibility of working in a particular business sector.

Finally there is *disengagement*. The end of the project may mean the end of this particular piece of work, but there may be extension work, i.e. other projects you can carry out to the benefit of the client, or the continuation of the existing project to further levels. Anyhow, the experience of having worked together will have effected a change in the relationship between consultant and client, which should provide a good basis for further work in the future.

There are further remarks on closure at the end of this chapter.

TERMS OF REFERENCE SPECIFY THE PROJECT

If I say to you that I am going to deliver a table to you next Monday, you would have a reasonable idea of what you're going to get. By contrast, if I say to you that I am coming to deliver some consultancy work for you next Monday, you will have far less idea of what you will be getting.

Now, there are many kinds of table, so I could perhaps show you a picture of that which I am going to deliver. In a similar way, terms of reference are a way of describing what is involved in a consultancy project.

The phrase 'terms of reference' will be interpreted variously by different consultants. The Shorter Oxford Dictionary defines terms of reference as 'the terms which define the scope of an inquiry', and this is a good starting point. Like Humpty Dumpty in 'Through the Looking Glass', however, in this chapter I shall define it to mean what I want it to mean. In my definition, as we shall see, this is enlarged to cover the *how* and *why* of the project, as well as the deliverables at its conclusion.

Whereas terms of reference in this definition relate to the content of a project, terms of business relate to the commercial context; terms of business are dealt with in Chapter 8.

Both aspects are usually brought together in a proposal submitted to the client. The proposal is the basis of the contract between consultant and client; it provides the foundation for all that follows within a consultancy project. It lays out the expectations of the client and consultant of each other – an important aspect of managing client relationships (see Chapter 4).

Terms of reference need to be established clearly for every assignment. Usually they should be written to avoid misunderstandings but, as with any contract, they can be oral as well as written.

Exhibit 3.2 Terms of reference

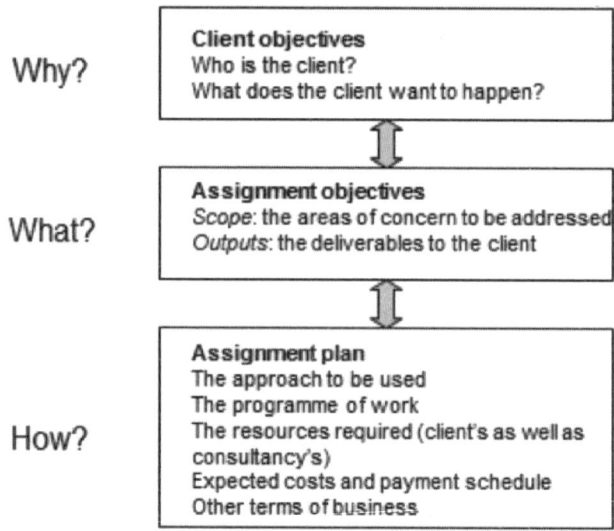

Exhibit 3.2 shows the framework for developing terms of reference. It consists of a statement of:
- the client objectives;
- the assignment objectives;
- the assignment plan.

These three relate together in a hierarchy of objectives: to go up the hierarchy you ask 'Why?', thus:
- *Why are we carrying out this plan?* To achieve the assignment objectives.
- *Why are we aiming at these assignment objectives?* To help the client achieve their objectives.

To go down the hierarchy, you ask 'How?', so:
- *How are the client's objectives to be achieved?* Through achieving the assignment objectives.
- *How are the assignment objectives to be achieved?* By means of the plan.

It is worth noting that usually there is only one answer to the question 'Why?', whereas there may be several answers to the question 'How?' What this means is that the consultancy assignment may be only one of several contributors to the client's objectives. The others, however, may not require consultancy support nor necessarily be in hand.

In the following sections we consider each of these three elements comprising terms of reference.

THE CLIENT'S OBJECTIVES

Consultants have to remember that their work is only a means to an end from the client's point of view. A consultant is (rightly) means-oriented whereas their client is ends-oriented. A consultant sees an assignment as a series of tasks, whereas a typical client sees it as a series of deliverables. But you should never lose sight of the context in which you are carrying out the assignment. To this end, you must remain aware who the client is and what the client wants to happen. This can sometimes be difficult when you are engrossed in the minutiae of a complex assignment. (Or, as someone once put it, 'When you're up to your ass in crocodiles, it's hard to remember you came to drain the swamp!')

It is essential to know who the real client is. If we call the person who is dealing with the consultant 'the sponsor' of the project, it is important to know if the sponsor is the real client or if there is someone behind the sponsor who is pushing to carry out the project. In the case study on ICC shown in Chapter 2, for example, the sponsor for a consultancy project is the General Manager (GM). What we do not (yet) know is whether John Smith's visit is at the GM's behest or whether the GM has been pushed into this by a superior. Were the latter true, then this might have a fundamental influence on the GM's attitude to the project; would he, for example, be a reluctant client? If this were the case, John Smith might find the project more difficult – the GM might be unwilling to release resources, make his own time available, and so on.

So what the client wants can be considered at two levels – commercial and personal objectives.

Commercial objectives

These will ultimately relate to:
- improving the performance of the existing business;
- improving its competitive position;
- developing new business.

Obviously the client's objectives for a particular project may not be phrased as these; nevertheless, it can be helpful to consultant and client alike to make explicit the causality between the commercial objective as framed and those stated above. This is easy to do in the case of ICC: the client wants to reduce product costs so the company's competitive position and profitability improve.

But what of assignments that are related less directly to commercial objectives – for example, carrying out a job evaluation project, helping with an office relocation or delivering a training course? In these cases tracking the client's objectives back to see how they relate to commercial objectives should help fashion the project so that it is more helpful to the client.

Personal objectives

These are just as relevant. The project sponsor will like the assignment to help them to do the job better, to run a better, more efficient department or business, to reflect to their credit and so on. Similarly, the sponsor will want to be sure the assignment doesn't go wrong and is not seen as an expensive waste of time. For this latter reason, a key dimension of a consultant's early contact with a sponsor is confidence building.

So there are general objectives that we can ascribe to the client at the start of a project.

There may also be specific ones. The consultancy salesperson may have to probe to find these. 'What are the client's unwritten objectives?' should be an item on the checklist of points that the salesperson ought to cover in briefing the operating team. There may be other requirements in terms of the conduct of the assignment:
- The extent to which the sponsor is to be involved in the detail;
- Freedom of access to other parts of the organisation (does everything have to be cleared through the sponsor?);
- The sponsor's wish to be involved in helping the development of ideas (e.g. does the sponsor want to be used as a sounding board, or receive considered views only?)

All this is about setting and understanding expectations which affect the client relationship. You need to establish a sound *modus operandi* with the client, which means understanding them personally as well as in their business role.

THE ASSIGNMENT OBJECTIVES

In Exhibit 3.2, the assignment objectives are defined by scope and outputs:
- The *scope* defines the areas of concern that are to be addressed;
- The *outputs* are what the client is going to get in respect of each of these areas – the deliverables.

Obviously these two together define the amount of work that an assignment might involve. The broader the scope, then the greater amount of work that eventually may be involved. Definition of the deliverables is equally important, particularly because they reflect the depth of analysis that is required to meet them. An in-depth study may need ten times the work of a 'quick and dirty' review.

It is essential that consultant and client have the same view of these two items. A career limiting factor in consultancy is to put yourself in a position where you have to do unpaid work because you have overrun your budget. This happens when a client has been promised a deliverable which the consultancy has not achieved within the given budget, or when there has been a misunderstanding over the scope of the assignment. For example, one consultancy agreed to do a study of the manufacturing facilities of a client, believing that there was only one factory site. In fact, there were three; additional resources were therefore required to complete the study.

If you find it difficult to define the scope of the assignment, then you are probably dealing with a 'messy' problem. Some preliminary work may therefore be required in order for the scope to be defined. The assignment therefore has to be broken into phases, the output of each phase defining the scope for the next. This is exemplified in Exhibit 3.3 which shows the scope and deliverables for the different levels of intervention in a consultancy project. (The idea of 'levels of intervention' was introduced in Chapter 2.)

Exhibit 3.3 Scope and deliverables for each level of intervention

Level	Scope	Outputs
1	Sense of organisational malaise	Purposes defined
2	How to achieve the purposes	Main problems that impede their achievement
3	How to resolve defined problems	How they can be best resolved
4	Implementation	Solutions put in place

For example, in the case of ICC, (the case study in Chapter 2), we assume that the objective of reducing high product costs has already been confirmed, so there is no need to start at level 1. At level 2, John Smith has to verify what the causes of high product costs might be – based on the clues he has found during his initial tour and his previous industry experience.

At the end of the work at this level he should have identified the problems causing high production costs; the level 3 intervention would be to decide how these might be best resolved.

At the start John Smith can only guess what solutions need to be implemented to reduce production costs. The terms of reference, therefore, cannot be comprehensive – he cannot prescribe (other than in the most general terms) what the outcome of the level 3 intervention will be, because the outputs of level 2 set the scope for level 3. He can therefore give firm terms of reference only for his work at level 2. The client may, however, require an estimate of fees for work from identifying the issues through to implementing the solutions. How to deal with this difficulty is dealt with in Chapter 8 under 'What do we tell the client?'

Make sure that each item identified within the scope has an output associated with it. An item in the scope with no output raises the question, 'How are you going to address this for the client?' An output unrelated to the scope usually implies:
- the output is related to part of the scope that has not been articulated, in which case the scope should be revised;
- the output is not required (for example, a consultant may produce an assignment report that is primarily for consumption within the consultancy practice instead of being a material means of advancing the performance of the client) in which case you should consider not producing the output.

Try to define outputs in terms which show how they relate to the client's objectives. 'So what?' analysis can be helpful here – ask 'So what?' of each output to see whether it relates to the client objective. (This is particularly useful when tempted to produce outputs consisting only of data feedback.)

Exhibit 3.4 shows the scope and outputs for ICC for interventions at level 2 and 3.

Exhibit 3.4 Assignment objectives

Level	Scope	Outputs
2	How can production costs be reduced?	The major issues resulting in high product costs identified
3	Wastage and rework rates	Report on how to reduce them
	Machine downtime	Recommend improved maintenance schedule
	Customer expectations of quality	Recommended changes to product specifications
	Suppliers' prices	Recommendations on improved purchasing policies and procedures

At the start of his assignment, John Smith has accepted the purpose that product costs have to be reduced, but can only guess what areas need to be tackled to reduce them. At the end of the level 2 intervention, therefore, his output is a more focused view of the areas that might be investigated in more detail.

Suppose at the end of this intervention he has identified the items shown in Exhibit 3.4 as the problems causing high production costs. At the next level of intervention (level 3) the deliverables could be the reports and recommendations shown in the figure. If he were then to help the client with a level 4 intervention, he would support the implementation of his recommendations.

I used to be worried that the output that a consultant produces so often consists of reports and recommendations – hardly a material intervention into the client environment. But given that a consultant rarely has executive authority within a client, outputs for action or a decision are usually expressed in terms of recommendations. Of course, the skill of the consultant lies in not only making the recommendations, but also in getting them accepted. (See later in this chapter.)

Although consultants can forecast outputs (i.e. immediate deliverables), they should be more conservative when forecasting outcomes or results. If the consultancy has total control of the factors influencing outcomes, then they can be more confident of predicting what the results of an assignment might be. Usually, however, a consultancy assignment is a joint activity between consultant and client, and so the results will depend on the co-operation and skill of the client staff, and the vagaries of the business environment. For these reasons, it is unusual for a consultancy to be able to guarantee the results of a project in terms of – say – decreased costs or increased performance. If it were rash enough to do so, and the expected results were not achieved, the client might reasonably claim some sort of redress.

What is most helpful under these circumstances is for the consultancy to indicate conditionally what the outcomes might be. 'Given the co-operation of your staff, we would expect costs to be reduced by 5–10 per cent', or 'Based on our experience elsewhere, we would expect this programme to increase the department's performance by at least 5 per cent'. These statements do not guarantee the results will be achieved; even so, some consultancies would prefer to use phrasing that is more non-committal. They may also have a disclaimer in their terms of business such as that reproduced below:

Forecasts, etc. by the Consultant

The time taken to complete the work and the measure of its success depend in part on factors outside the control of the Consultant. These include the degree of co-operation given by the Client's staff and promptness in agreeing and implementing recommendations. Any forecast or estimate made by the consultant of the time required for the assignment and the results attainable is given in good faith having regard to the information made available by the Client and represents the Consultant's interpretations of the Client's instructions. Any such estimates and any confirmation or variation of them in subsequent reports and correspondence shall not be deemed in any circumstances to be undertakings, warranties or contractual conditions.

(Source: Institute of Management Consultancy)

ASSIGNMENT PLAN

The items shown in the box 'Assignment plan' in Exhibit 3.2 can themselves be related in a hierarchy of objectives thus:

How are we going to implement this approach?
... By carrying out this programme of work.
How are we going to carry out this programme of work?
... By utilising these resources.
The hierarchy can again be ascended by asking the question 'Why?'

Resources may be drawn from both client and consultant. It is essential that the client recognises the resources they must provide, both in the conduct of the assignment and its management (see below). And, of course, the consultancy will be providing resources for a price; this price, with the other aspects relating to the commercial context of the business, will be embodied in the terms of business – see Chapter 8.

Deciding the method of approach

This is the means by which you get from the areas of concern to the ways in which they can be best addressed – the deliverables. The approach to be used relies on an appraisal of how the consultancy team and client are respectively to contribute to the achievement of the project objectives. From this appraisal all the work on the assignment is predicated. As a consultant, you must be clear about what you are bringing to the party.

This will determine what your role is, and it has to be complementary to that of the client. At one extreme you can be highly interventionist and take much of the project onto your own shoulders. At the other extreme, the role of the consultant is facilitative, enabling the client to address the problem for themselves. Between these two extremes is a spectrum of consultancy roles, and you must decide which is appropriate.

Some projects are handed over to the consultant by the client and there is no further contact until the work is complete. Such projects are often research oriented. For example, a client might ask a consultant to identify the size of market and buying criteria for a product in Zambia. The consultant would carry out the research and then report to the client.

For the most part, however, projects are co-operative efforts between consultant and client. Even in a research oriented project a consultant will probably have some reviews with the client between beginning and end. For instance, in the ICC case study, the GM will probably arrange for John Smith to have access to records, people, equipment and other resources, to enable him to diagnose the key problems (the level 2 intervention). John Smith will engage in data collection and report back with his conclusions.

In the next phase, he will need to decide how the problems he has identified should be addressed, which may entail the active involvement of some of ICC's staff. They might, for example, engage in data collection, contribute their ideas, or plan operational improvements. Different modes of client and consultant working together can therefore be involved even in a simple project.

The next consideration in deciding the method of approach concerns the perception of the nature of the predicament. A client may see the issues to be dealt with in more simple terms than the consultant and would therefore not be in favour of an approach that treated it as complicated. In the example of ICC, the GM might see the problems of product cost being entirely due to poor quality production. He may even have employed John Smith to come up with the conclusion that high product costs are entirely the result of poor equipment performance, and to use this as a lever for winning capital investment from his head office.

No consultant will retain the goodwill of a client by speaking against the client's favourite ideas on day one. Remember the dictum 'Sell the client what they need in terms of what they want'; the consultant has to educate the client into the true nature of the issues that have to be addressed. The client's perception of these may therefore develop throughout the course of a project. This does not mean active opposition. If you set up an 'either/or' situation (either your view prevails, or mine) then you will lose – certainly in the long term. You should establish a 'both/and' view, i.e. 'we will investigate both your ideas and others, which from the evidence and our experience, we believe will help to achieve your objective.' The client can be brought round to the consultant's view – if appropriate - later in the project.

A further point you must consider when deciding the method of approach occurs when a client is embarking on a project which represents a significant change to the business. You need to know whether the problem solving processes available within the client's organisation are appropriate for dealing with this problem. For example, there are some organisations in which most of the transactions are oral and face to face – little is written down. One such was a business in which the founder and owner was a 'dealer' – an entrepreneur who had built the business on his skills in striking good deals. The method of problem solving in the business derived from this process: problems were resolved at a round table discussion culminating with a 'deal' – who was going to do what. While this approach was effective for many operational problems in the business, it was less effective in coping with more complex problems of a strategic nature. The consultant had to educate the client in other methods of problem solving, by setting up a working party to study the issues and helping the client use a multistage approach to dealing with them.

In summary, therefore, in deciding the method of approach, the consultant has to consider:
- What are the skills and resources consultant and client can respectively bring to solving this problem?
- What is the client's expectation of the consultant's role and how appropriate is this?

- What is the client's view of the problem, and how does it differ from that of the consultant?
- What is the nature of the predominant problem solving procedures within the client?
- What are the skills and resources the client can bring to solving this problem?

Programme of work

Once the method of approach has been established, the programme of work explains what is going to happen and when. This is in effect the assignment plan. Sometimes clients find it difficult to visualise how the consultancy will accomplish the assignment objectives. The assignment plan helps by showing how the transition is to be made from the present situation to the new one. It is therefore a good way of building a client's confidence in the project.

Project planning

There is often a reluctance to plan, but planning is vital if projects are to be delivered on time, good client relationships are to be preserved and budgeted time and resources are not to be exceeded. One reason for this reluctance is that planning can be difficult in complex situations, or at the start of a project when there are a lot of unknowns. In such circumstances, it is sensible to break a project into a number of stages, each dependent on the findings of the former. The use of explicit planning assumptions can also be helpful in dealing with this. As the project progresses, the validity of these assumptions can be tested and the plan modified in the light of any revised assumptions.

Project planning should start during the bidding process for a project, when it will be necessary to estimate the time and other resources required to carry out the project. The elements of a project plan will consist of:

- a breakdown of the deliverables to be produced by the project, derived from the project objectives;
- a breakdown of the project into the tasks or work packages required to produce these deliverables;
- a logic diagram showing the sequence and dependencies of these tasks;
- the resources required for each task.

When the start date for the project has been confirmed, two other elements have to be added:

- A list of the specific individuals (from whatever source) who will work on the project, with exact details of their availability both in terms of the number of hours a week they will be working, and the dates when they will be unavailable;
- A timetable showing when each activity will be done, and who will do it.

If the project consists of a number of phases, a plan will need to be prepared for each phase.

In addition to other elements involved, every project plan should include:
- *Milestones* at which the progress of a project can be assessed.
- *Formal progress reviews* attended by the project manager, the account manager and the client. (Informal progress reviews may take place more frequently.) These should coincide at least with milestones, and may be held more frequently.
- *Schedule of deliverables*: When deliverables (e.g. reports) are to be produced for the client.
- *Invoicing schedule*: When the client is to be invoiced for the project.

With projects of any complexity (involving a number of consultants), time should be allowed in the project plan for project administration, such as briefing and review meetings with consultants, as well as team maintenance activities.

Consultancy is a practical skill that is developed therefore on the job. One of the responsibilities of a project manager is not only to deliver the assignment promises but also to support members of the project team (not only from the consultancy but also those seconded from the client) in their personal development. This requires consultation with them on their personal learning objectives at the outset of the project and seeking opportunities to help them get the experience needed during the course of their work on the project.

Resources required

The programme of work will specify the tasks needed to be carried out by the consultant team, and hence the resources the consultancy has to provide. The fees that are charged to the client will be related to the cost of the assignment. This in turn will be based on an estimate of the time required from each consultant multiplied by their fee rate. The accuracy of the estimate of the time required is thus central to the profitability (or otherwise) of a consultancy project.

If there are a number of people engaged in a project, a 'Time and Responsibilities Schedule', should be issued on a regular basis showing:
- the tasks to be accomplished;
- who is responsible for each task;
- the resources (time, other) to be devoted to the task;
- when the task has to be complete.

A schedule may cover only those tasks in the immediate future; further schedules can be issued as a project progresses.

It is worth making explicit the resources you will need from a client to carry out an assignment. Sometimes these are clear – for example, when a member of client staff is to be assigned to the project team – but there are other workload implications for a client embarking on a consultancy assignment. For example, the client resources a consultant might need are accommodation, access to the client's intranet or Wi-Fi, use of administrative support (e.g. for fixing meetings) and other office services. The consultant will also need time from the sponsor to carry out progress reviews. There may also be more active involvement of client staff – responding to interviews and questionnaires, or communicating aspects of the project to staff within the organisation.

How the project is to be organised

All projects require some input from clients, if only to act as a reporting link. More is usually required, e.g. to take decisions. Not all clients are accustomed to using consultants and it may be necessary to advise a client on the appropriate organisation to manage the project internally.

A question that consultant and client need to debate is, 'Can this project be managed within the ordinary processes of management, or does it require extra-ordinary arrangements for its management?' In the latter case (which happens more often than not) special arrangements need to be made.

Managerial and other resources required from a client should be made clear at a project's inception. The consultant should also comment on the organisation structure that the client should establish for dealing with the project. The simplest structure applies when a consultant reports directly to the sponsor of the project. At the other extreme is a major project being run by an organisation, in which the consultancy firm is making a sub-contractor's contribution within an established organisation structure.

Between these two extremes lies the project steering group. This can consist of the consultancy project manager and the client sponsor, plus other members. The selection of other members is significant. If senior members of departments affected by the project are co-opted onto the steering committee, they should provide helpful counsel, and their participation should help to get better acceptance of any changes proposed. A steering committee also gets a broader exposure for the consultancy firm, and reduces its vulnerability to reliance on a single sponsor.

Obviously there are many variations on this theme such as a project steering group that reports to a more senior committee, or subgroups that are responsible for particular aspects of the project.

Consultancy practices will have had more experience of dealing with consultancy projects than their clients, and therefore should always consider what is the most appropriate form of client organisation. In some circumstances this may mean challenging the project organisation that the client may have in place already. Having said that, however, the increasing size of the consulting sector means that a large number of executives may have had previous experience of working in a consulting practice and may therefore be well able to shape a project organisation for a consulting intervention.

DIAGNOSIS: MANAGING CONSULTANCY PROJECTS

Having set up the consultancy project, much of the work then involves problem solving and data collection – topics already covered in Chapter 2. In this section we consider how the project itself is to be managed during its course.

Consultancy work is mostly project based so all consultants have to have skills in project management. At one end of the project spectrum is the project of perhaps only a few days carried out by a single consultant. At the other is the major project of a year or more involving a large team of consultants, sub-contractors and so on. All demand skills of project management.

The effectiveness with which a project is executed will depend in large measure on the quality of project management. It is not the purpose of this text to provide a comprehensive treatise on project management; there are several standard methodologies available, some of which are used by consultancy practices. Whether or not you are using a standard project management system, however, from the point of view of managing the practice, you need to be assured that project management is being carried out to an appropriate standard of performance.

We have already considered the project plan under terms of reference above. The plan provides a forecast of activity and resources. Without a plan, it is impossible to monitor how things are going and thereby to take corrective action when required.

PRINCIPLES OF PROJECT PLANNING AND CONTROL

I find the metaphor of a journey a useful one to gain an insight into the key components of a project.

In planning a journey you have to know where you are going and when you need to be there. You must decide what route you are to take, which means that you need to know where you're starting from and whether there are any limitations on the route you can take. (For example, is the aim to take the fastest route, the prettiest route, or the most economical? Do you need to make a detour to pick some people up on the way?) You will need to make sure that you have the right resources for your trip (Are you going by car or another form of transport? Will you need to take food?).

Suppose that you are to travel from London to Bristol by road, to arrive in Bristol at a specific time. If you are to be able to control the implementation of your plan, you need to monitor how you are doing; you need to have 'milestones', so that at predetermined points on your route, say Reading and Swindon, you can judge whether you are ahead or behind schedule, and act appropriately. You will also need to be able to tell when you have arrived in Bristol.

On your journey you may have to change your plans because a road might be closed, or there is a severe traffic jam. Indeed, there may be a radio report that causes you to decide to change your destination; you are going to Bristol for a holiday, but reports of bad weather make you decide to go to Exeter instead. Plans may therefore need to change to take account of changed circumstances.

From the metaphor of a journey, you can infer the important features of project planning and control for a consultant:

- You have to know the purpose of the project and why the client wants it done. The deliverables from the project and the timing of their delivery must be defined, stated and agreed.
- You need to decide what steps are involved in achieving the project objectives, and what, if any, subsidiary objectives might affect this plan.
- You need to ensure you have the resources required.
- If you are to be able to control the project, you need to programme in some milestones, i.e. points during the project at which you can judge progress. It is too late to wait until the end to ask, 'Did we make it?'
- No business stands still; during the course of a project of any duration a business will have moved on. It is therefore probable that the detailed requirements of the project will also change.

Other aspects of this metaphor are also helpful; for example, to go on a journey you have to leave your point of departure. Sometimes client staff don't want to leave the past behind, but there will be no progress unless they do.

Project control

Project control is the process of monitoring actual activity and events against those projected in the project plan. It follows that if the plan is poor, control will be more difficult – control can be only as good as the plan itself.

The project manager should maintain records of:
- dates when tasks and phases have been completed;
- dates when deliverables have been made to the client;
- the consumption of time and fees and other resources against budget;
- any other aspects relating to the management of the quality of the project.

If several consultants are involved in a project, the project manager must gather this information regularly from each member of the project team.

It is often useful for the project manager (and consultants in the project team) to keep a 'project diary' - a notebook in which all information relating

to the project can be kept. This includes notes of telephone calls, meetings, key decisions and so on. A project diary is particularly necessary when working on projects that are deemed risky. The commercial aspects of risk are dealt with in Chapter 8; there are also operating risks, which occur in the following situations:
- Where the project is complex, or depends on innovative techniques;
- Where a major section of the client staff is antagonistic to the project;
- Where the client is unreliable, e.g. in not providing resources as promised;
- Where the project is politically sensitive;
- Where the consultancy resources are likely to be overstretched;
- Where the terms of reference are ill-defined, or likely to change during the project.

The project manager should exercise control through progress reviews. A progress review should be held at each milestone, or more frequently, as set out in the plan. The progress review should cover:
- progress: achievements to date and use of resources, compared with budget;
- problems, actual or anticipated;
- plans, including short-term action, addressing problems, and rescheduling tasks.

This may be summarised in a progress report, which might in addition comment on:
- key meetings held with staff;
- opportunities for further work following on from the project.

The project manager should conclude the report with an overall appraisal of project progress and the state of the client relationship.

During the course of a project, circumstances change and more information becomes available, and so plans made at the start of a project may no longer be appropriate. Replanning should therefore be regarded as the rule, not the exception with projects extending more than several months. Project plans should be amended accordingly. Re-planning may influence two important factors:
- the scheduling of resources;
- the ability to honour commitments made to clients.

Managing expectations is an important component of maintaining a good client relationship (see Chapter 4). If re-planning is necessary, consider what the impact of this will be on the client, and how they should be best kept informed.

Keeping the client informed

Client expectations have to be carefully managed, and this must be done through regular contacts with the client. Progress reviews with the client should form part of the project plan.

It is particularly important to make sure that the client is kept well informed during the early stages of a project. This is the period when the client may feel more insecure if nothing is heard; frequent reassurance that all is going to plan will build the confidence of the client. The policy with clients should be 'No surprises'.

It is a feature of consultancy projects that things occasionally go wrong, perhaps through unfortunate circumstances, accident, failure of a consultant or client, or simply because individuals do not get on. These situations can be managed and rectified only if they are recognised and dealt with before they become crises. Very often the consultant can handle them alone; on other occasions more help may be required. This can be provided only if the consultant says that help is needed.

Similarly, client confidence is bolstered by achievements, and so these should be publicised to the client whenever appropriate.

Changing terms of reference

When engaged in the detail of a project, it is easy to lose sight of the project objectives, let alone why the client commissioned it. The terms of reference should be referred to frequently, to ensure the project keeps on track.

It is not unusual for terms of reference to change during a project. This may be because circumstances have changed, or because new information has become available which means that the scope or outputs of the project should change.

It is important that the same rigour of thinking goes into revised terms of reference as in the original. Again, it is essential that client and consultant have expectations in common. Consequently, it is sensible to secure the client's agreement and to document any changes.

This is particularly important if the original terms of reference are written. Although changes might be orally agreed, a change of job incumbent or deterioration in the client relationship may require there to be evidence of the agreed change.

In such circumstances, therefore:
- The implications of the change on the existing project should be assessed.
- The change and its implications should be discussed and agreed with the client.
- The change should be documented, in particular noting changes in deliverables, timescales and fees.

As mentioned above, clients' circumstances change over time, so on longer projects changing terms of reference should not be regarded as unusual.

INTERVENTION: DEVELOPING AND IMPLEMENTING RECOMMENDATIONS

Intervention is the culmination of a consultancy project, which usually means getting recommendations accepted. By recommendations I mean not only substantive advice from the consultant as an expert, but also suggestions about processes in which a client might engage, with the consultant in a supporting role.

Implementation of a consultant's recommendations is often in two parts:
- The translation of recommendations into decisions, which is done at an executive level in an organisation;
- The translation of recommendations (or decisions) into action, which may be done at more junior levels – or more simply, implementation.

Intervention is discussed in these two respects later in this chapter, but first, we need to consider how to formulate high quality recommendations.

Consultants are occasionally likened to giant birds that fly into an organisation, excrete a fat report, and then fly off again. Obviously there will be occasions when this is just what is wanted. But if the intention is to do something more, failure may be the result of poor recommendations.

FORMULATING HIGH QUALITY RECOMMENDATIONS

So, what makes for high quality recommendations? There are three criteria to be considered:
- Technical adequacy – will they work?
- Acceptability to the client;
- The capacity of the client to implement them – their do-ability.

Technical adequacy
This criterion is the most familiar and straightforward: will the recommendations help the client to address the project objectives satisfactorily? Given that the purpose of a consultancy assignment is to do just this, then I hope that the answer is 'Yes'. If in doubt, refer to the terms of reference!

Every assignment should have a spice of originality to the recommendations. No two clients are identical, and so it is unlikely that identical recommendations will be suitable. And, if they are, it should be because alternatives have been considered and abandoned. Indeed, some clients will find it helpful to know of the options that have been eliminated and the reasons for this.

Most consultants come to the profession having their roots in some sort of specialised knowledge. So, for example, a marketing consultant will probably have both some formal, academic grounding in the topic as well as previous experience, perhaps, in an executive role in marketing. As a subject matter expert they may arrive at recommendations that will be excellent for the client, but these may need to be compromised in order to meet the remaining criteria – acceptability and do-ability.

Acceptability

A consultant will often need to work hard to get their recommendations accepted and implemented by a client. But if a recommendation is profoundly unacceptable – not in the interests of the client or of influential members of client staff – then compromise is necessary. For example, a consultancy team advising on organisational issues took the view that the newly appointed Chief Executive was the wrong person to lead a particular client forward. The ideal recommendation was to replace him, but soundings showed there was insufficient support for this among the other directors. The compromise was to strengthen the executive team so that the Chief Executive would have adequate support in carrying out the tasks in the areas in which he was weakest.

Acceptability will also be conditional on the culture and values of the organisation. For instance, there may be 'rules' about how change may be introduced; for instance, 'no redundancies'.

So you can define a 'state of readiness' of a client for recommendations of different kinds. The reality, however, is that this is rarely dispersed uniformly across the organisation. Frequently, there are differences at various levels of management; top management, for example, embraces structural change as a means of performance development, while middle management – who perhaps see the disadvantages more clearly – are often more reserved.

Do-ability

The history of foreign aid to less developed countries abounds in stories of well-meaning donations of sophisticated equipment that cannot be repaired when it breaks down, because of a lack of spare parts, or there is no infrastructure to distribute them, or insufficient skill to fit them properly. From this difficulty arose the notion of intermediate technology – not the most advanced, but that which a recipient country can sustain.

Similar considerations apply to clients: their organisations may be unable to sustain the 'best' technical solution. The consultant may install it, and it works well for a while, but at the first sign of difficulty the new system breaks

down irretrievably as far as the client is concerned. So again compromise may be necessary. Points for consideration are:
- Has the client got the necessary resources – managerial, financial – to sustain this solution?
- Has the client got the skills (technical, systems) to support this solution?
- Is this solution consistent with the client's culture and style of management? Solutions that require a fundamental change in client culture or behaviour are more susceptible to failure.

TRANSLATING RECOMMENDATIONS INTO DECISIONS

Having got high quality recommendations adopted by executives, will they be translated into decisions? Whether they are accepted depends on two factors:
- The consultant's influence, which will affect the weight that the client attaches to what the consultant says;
- The attractiveness (or otherwise) of the specific recommendations.

If a consultant's view carries little weight, then it will be difficult for them to get recommendations accepted irrespective of how sound they are.

This is not only about how to present recommendations to best effect. Recommendations are like tender young plants: the ground has to be prepared carefully beforehand if they are to flourish. Similarly, the conduct of the assignment must provide a basis for the warm reception of the recommendations.

The nature of a consultant's influence

First, therefore, let us consider the nature of a consultant's influence.

By definition, consultants have no legitimate executive authority within the client organisation. Sometimes they may have delegated authority; members of client staff may be assigned to work under their direction on a consultancy project, but this authority will be within strict confines. For the most part, however, a consultant can only influence rather than mandate the decision making processes within a client.

So what power does the consultant have? It is the consultant's expertise – knowledge, skill, experience, know-how – that gains them admission into a client organisation. If you do not have expertise, then you cannot act as an expert. Once inside an organisation, another type of power also comes into play – connection power. The consultant will often have been appointed by executives more senior than the client staff with whom the consultant is working on a day to day basis. Connection power gives a power of sanction – if junior staff are not co-operative, then the consultant can use connections at a senior level to make things happen. Because of the connection with key people, the consultant may come into possession of information about situations, plans and so on, which is not generally known. This can help in planning how to exert influence. Moreover, client staff may pay more heed to consultants if they believe that they are privy to, and have an influence over, their future careers.

It is the perception of power that leads to influence; for example, irrespective of how skilled you are, if you are not credited with any expertise, you will have no expert power. You therefore need to make careful efforts to develop your influence by:
- using your expertise for cultivating connections within the client;
- using these connections to exercise influence.

Your behaviour will also determine the degree of influence you have. Consider:
- *How do you see yourself?* People will initially take you at your own valuation. If you have a low opinion of yourself, your abilities, or your standing with the client, this will come across. Consultants should not be arrogant, but neither are they supplicants.
- *What impression do you make?* From day one of their career, consultants are taught that first impressions count. It is a point so well known that it may not seem worthwhile repeating, yet it still creates difficulties. So remember that your appearance, what you say, and how you comport yourself, will affect the impression that you make. And be natural – clients are offended if you try to pretend to be something that you're not.
- *How do you and your colleagues treat one another?* If you treat one another with disdain, what is the client to make of this? For example, there was a director of a consultancy who was introducing a young consultant to a client. During the meeting, the director peremptorily asked his colleague to fetch his briefcase from his car. Although the director was undoubtedly the senior, he had undermined the standing of his junior colleague with that client from the start.

Optimising expert power

For the most part, a consultant starts with a fund of expert power – an expectation that they are expert in their area of specialisation. What the consultant says or does enhances or diminishes this. The wrong appearance or asking foolish questions revealing a lack of knowledge will undermine the perception of the consultant's expertise.

The perception of expert power will derive not only from what the consultant says and does, but also from:
- *The label of 'consultant'*. Being labelled a consultant is not always a passport to friendly acceptance by client staff. Negative feelings can arise from consultancy projects in the past that have led to painful change, previous experience of poor quality consultancy service or

dislike of the consultant's role, fee rate, etc. Nevertheless, the label of consultant should create an expectation of having at least some expertise.
- *The 'source effect' of the consultant's firm.* 'Source effect' is the equivalent of the branding of the consultancy firm; it derives from its reputation. If the consultant works for a practice that is known to the client, they will take on some of the attributes of that consultancy.

Developing expert power comes by displaying technical expertise. This must be complemented by understanding. Airing technical knowledge is unlikely to impress a client; applying technical knowledge to a client's problems in a helpful way, and explaining this in terms the client understands will help to enhance your influence.

Optimising connection power

Connection power derives from contact with important or influential members of client staff, so it is important therefore that a consultant preserves connections with them. For example, the mechanism of a steering committee can be used in project management to maintain contacts with senior people, and to escalate the level and range of contacts within an organisation.

Maintaining appropriate contacts within the client organisation is, in effect, networking – a concept that we will meet in connection with selling. In this instance the consultant is trying to 'sell' themselves within the client organisation.

To this end, you should seek to establish and maintain a variety of links within the client organisation. Every interaction with the client will affect how you are perceived. While preparing for meetings, interviews, presentations or any other interaction, therefore, you must consider not only the business of the meeting, but also how it might be used to develop your influence in the client.

For example, suppose that at the start of an assignment you have to collect information from each director on the client's board. This provides an excellent opportunity for the consultant to form relationships with the key executives in the client organisation. The risk is that the consultant sees this as solely data collection, thereby missing this opportunity.

EXERCISING INFLUENCE

So far we have been considering the nature of a consultant's influence – the accretion of expert and connection power, so that when they speak, what is said commands at least some attention.

Next, we need to consider the exercise of this influence, so as to secure adoption of particular recommendations. Getting recommendations adopted starts long before their presentation, and entails managing informal as well as formal communications with the client.

Informal communications

All interactions with a client are interventions into the client environment, and have to be managed as such. For example in an interview programme, the consultant might start the process of change by asking a single question. For example, 'Has the company ever considered moving to a lower cost location?' might prompt this consideration if none had previously been given.

It is often useful to get reaction to ideas well before presenting them, during progress reviews and other meetings or encounters with key executives. You can float them without commitment: 'One of the suggestions that has been made is...', or, 'We came across this idea at another client's...' Discussing the way your thinking is going can also elicit useful information that can help you in reformulating or refining recommendations.

Formal communications

Formal communications will consist of face to face presentations and meetings, and reports and other written communications. The choice of to whom to communicate is important. Key influencers within the organisation are an obvious choice, but remember:
- You may not have direct access to them; you may therefore need to deal (at least initially) with connectors who act as gatekeepers to them.
- The power to say 'No' is widely distributed throughout an organisation. Although someone may not be able to make something happen, they may be able to stop it. So remember you will need to convince those who can stop a proposal as well as those who can make it happen.

Matching communication style with the decision making style of the organisation

Also important is choosing an appropriate style of communication.

The style with which an organisation takes decisions is on a spectrum from action oriented to reflective. Organisations with an action-oriented style will like face to face communications. They will appreciate being presented with the key points and will aim to sort out what has to be done at a single meeting. By contrast, those organisations with a reflective style will prefer to receive a paper on a topic, which is then discussed at a committee meeting.

Working with each has its pros and cons. The action-oriented like to get things done quickly. The disadvantage is that this does not work when dealing with complex problems. For example, one professional services firm was reviewing how it could best develop its business in the midst of a recession.

The approach among partners was for each to assert what the solution was and seek to persuade their colleagues of it. This did not allow any effort to be put into thinking about what the nature of the problem was, and so the action taken was not particularly effective.

The reflective style does allow debate about the nature of the problem, but it can also be frustrating for an action-oriented organisation. For example, a financial services group was considering restructuring its bonus plan, which had profound implications for their (very strong) culture. The consultant sought to explore the issues by presenting a series of papers to a steering committee. The steering committee wanted more speedy action, and so became increasingly frustrated, until the work reached the implementation stage. Here, the consultant had failed to match the required style; a more action-oriented approach was required.

This difference of style applies to individuals, too, who can be action-oriented, or reflective, or somewhere between the two. The consultant needs to suit the manner of communication to the style. Papers will be read only cursorily by the action-oriented, while a reflective manager will not like to make a decision of any moment without a paper being presented on the topic first.

One of a consultant's functions is educative, leaving clients better able to deal with the matters of concern addressed on the assignment (see 'Transfer' later in this chapter). The consultant may need to educate the client in different methods of decision making, so that the issues may be dealt with effectively. In so doing, you have to be careful not to be so countercultural as to be rejected.

TRANSLATING RECOMMENDATIONS INTO ACTION

The challenges for a consultant in turning recommendations into action are:
- Getting recommendations accepted by those affected and gaining their commitment.
- Managing the change process.
- Ensuring that the client has an ongoing capability to support the change after implementation, so that transfer takes place.

Gaining commitment

Although in theory it is possible to demand compliance with a change, positive commitment from those affected will yield better results. The following will help to build commitment.
- *Changes should be owned and supported by the client organisation.* Any change should be seen as an initiative being taken by the client organisation rather than being identified with the consultants. Active and visible support from top management is required. Giving the project a name can also help (e.g. a TQM (total quality management)

project might be entitled 'Project Gold'). This conclusion is supported by research, which shows that change programmes frequently fail to deliver the results that were anticipated. The successful ones have one dominant feature: the active commitment and involvement of top management.

- *Participation leads to commitment.* People will become more committed if they are kept informed and participate in decisions. The sooner this starts, the better. It may not be possible to involve everybody from the start (e.g. before a decision has been made to proceed), but thereafter involvement should be more than is usual. For example, although junior members of staff may not decide where their office is to be located, they might have a say in the layout and decor of where they work.

  More time and resources need to be allowed for communication during a change – existing communication arrangements may not be adequate by themselves. Similarly, there may need to be more participation in decision making. A useful technique here is 'reservations in the right to decide'. Rather than delegating specific decisions to those affected by the change, define those that they should not make, and then leave the remaining decisions to them.

- *Honour resistance.* Resistance is the opposite of commitment, and dealing with it usually means overcoming it. An alternative view is to honour it. This attaches a value to those who resist by assuming that they do so for what to them are sound reasons. These reasons could be germane to the success of the project, and ignoring them would be foolish.

There will be some people, however, who cannot make the change and therefore resist it irrationally and may eventually have to transfer job or leave the organisation if the change is to be implemented successfully.

Managing the change process

Implementing change is a process, and it is a process that has to be managed. The previous section on gaining commitment implied that change often involves new ways of communicating and taking decisions. Key points in managing a change process are:

- *Allow sufficient resources for carrying out the change.* Not only does the substance of change take time, but so too does the process. There is rarely enough organisational slack to enable people to undertake a major change while continuing with their existing level of work. Some reallocation of tasks to allow those involved the time to carry out the change is necessary, as well as support from outside consultants.
- *Launch the change.* Running some sort of event to mark the start of the change process can raise its profile and start the unfreezing

process. A training course, workshop, 'kick-off' meeting or similar event can be used.
- *Work with key people.* There will be key people on whom you should devote more time than the rest. You should identify who can make a major difference to the success or failure of the project (not everybody will) and spend a disproportionately large amount of time with them.
- *Nurse the change during the early stages.* There are bound to be teething problems with any change, and so more support is required during the early stages when people are learning the new ways. When trying anything new, performance falls (e.g. when a baby starts to walk, it makes less progress than when it crawled). People will need reassurance that this is to be expected, and does not mean that the change has failed.
- *Give feedback and celebrate success.* People need to know how they are doing; feedback is therefore particularly important during the change process. Celebrating major milestones marks the successful progress of change.
- *Make sure that psychological and material rewards do not act as a barrier to change.* People will be inhibited from changing if a bonus scheme, or the basis of performance appraisal, career progression, or simply what managers praise, is oriented to the old arrangements. You should therefore make sure that rewards are modified to be consistent with changed circumstances.

CLOSURE: COMPLETING THE PROJECT

TRANSFER

A key aspect of closure is transfer.

Transfer is the process of making sure the client has an ongoing capability to support the change after the consultant has gone. Methods of effecting transfer include:
- training;
- providing manuals and programmes;
- establishing systems and procedures.

Key points are:
- *Transfer is part of the project.* If consultant and other resources are not contracted for transfer, it won't happen. Transfer should be included, where appropriate, in the terms of reference and provisions should be made in the project costing for carrying it out.

- *Transfer should include follow-up.* Follow-up visits by the consultant can be used to ensure that transfer has been successful, and can be used to deal with any problems that might have cropped up.

A further advantage of follow-up is to consultants – it gives them a further right of entry to a client organisation, and therefore provides a commercial opportunity.

EVALUATION

Finally, there needs to be some sort of review of the project. At a superficial level, evaluation is simply assessing the degree to which the client was satisfied; but on a project of any significant size, you should carry out a case review which:
- identifies the key learnings arising from the project;
- records these on the practice's knowledge management system.

Case review can also be done jointly with the client – not only leading to richer results but in a growth in the relationship.

The capitalisation of intellectual property from operating experience is a key process in a consulting practice; consultants need to learn and profit from the experience of their colleagues. Closure processes are a means of achieving this.

4
MANAGING CLIENT RELATIONSHIPS

The Managing Director of a small family company was recounting his experiences with consultants over the previous ten years. 'My father started the business and, like many entrepreneurs, was very resistant to advice. It was only when we were approaching bankruptcy that we got in our first consultant – who saved us.

'Since then, our experience has been mixed. One consultant produced a report on meeting an industry standard, which was four times as thick as necessary. He simply duplicated what he'd done for his last client; it was a disaster. The next – a supply chain consultant – didn't tell us anything we didn't know already and failed to tell us some things we already knew.

'We had some craft training done by an outsider; that went well. We also got a consultant in to help us introduce a new payment scheme for all staff. Not only did he do this, but he also gave us a valuable report on our industrial relations.

'Later, we had a consultant from a highly reputable firm to advise us on our marketing. We had some specific questions to which we particularly wanted answers. The consultant didn't bother answering our questions. The only impact he had on our business was one of creating annoyance.'

It takes a lot of effort to win a client, but very little to lose them. Selling has often been likened to courtship; but after the client has been won, the eagerly courted girlfriend can become a neglected wife, who complains, 'You never bring me flowers anymore.' In one instance, a consultant promised a proposal to a new director of a long-standing client. Owing to pressure of other work, the consultant forgot his promise and failed to submit the proposal (a situation unique in my experience!) The director was so incensed that he persuaded his colleagues not to use the consultancy on any further projects whatsoever. The relationship was ruined, and the client completely lost.

It is likely that none of these consultants was technically incompetent and certain that those who upset their client did not intend to do so. Technical competence is not sufficient by itself; the client relationship has to be actively managed, and this is the topic of this chapter.

WHY THE CLIENT RELATIONSHIP IS IMPORTANT

A good client relationship yields considerably more benefits than simply the esteem of a satisfied client. Quite apart from the fact that it is easier and more pleasant to do business with a satisfied client, there are clear commercial advantages.

A GOOD RELATIONSHIP IS A DIFFERENTIATOR

Products and services can be based on the spectrum shown in Exhibit 4.1. At one end you have unique products; a famous painting might fall into this category.

Exhibit 4.1 A spectrum of products and services

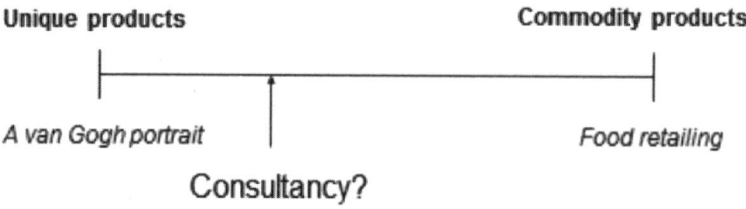

Fairly close to that end must be the monopoly suppliers of a product. At the other end are commodity products – those that change very little according to the supplier, and for which there are many suppliers. Food retailing is an example of this: there is no difference in a particular brand of soap powder according to the shop you buy it at.

Plainly a salesperson is in a lot stronger position when a product lies towards the left-hand side of the spectrum. The purpose of branding a product is to move from the right-hand side towards the left, by giving attributes to the product additional to the qualities of the product itself. At the simplest level this might be attractive packaging; in the service industry it is achieved by reputation and fashion.

From a client's point of view, the services offered by a consultancy firm are really undifferentiated products; how the services are delivered is therefore fundamental in creating a good reputation. The quality of a consultant's reputation is vital in getting new business. Positive recommendations from satisfied clients to others in their network are worth many hours of selling and marketing by the consultant. Conversely, there is much truth in the old adage, 'One bad job costs a hundred good ones.'

A GOOD RELATIONSHIP HELPS SALES

Former clients are perhaps the best source of further business, by asking the consultant to continue to provide services in a particular area of specialisation or by giving the consultancy practice the opportunity to provide a wider range of services, or recommending them to other organisations.

Conversely, few consultants can claim to have an invulnerable client base. Just as they will seek to enlarge the size of their businesses by acquiring the clients of their competitors, so too will their competitors themselves be attempting to do the same. A poor client relationship will make a client more open to an approach from a competing consultancy practice for future work.

THE CLIENT RELATIONSHIP MUST BE ACTIVELY MANAGED

It is tempting to believe that the quality of client relationships is simply the result of luck or happenstance. This is not true. The client relationship must be actively managed in a way complementary to the technical work being carried out by the consultant. Consultants must bring competence to both these tasks if they are to be truly effective.

Consultants have taken up their specialisation because of their interest in the topic. Their training is directed towards achieving excellence in the technical aspects of their work. But the judgement made by clients about the quality of a consultant will not be simply on the technical aspects of their work together; it will also depend on a variety of other factors that contribute to the nature of their mutual relationship. For example, the consultant who carries out a project to a high standard but takes too long over it will leave a trail of discontented clients.

Client relationships rarely deteriorate because consultants think them unimportant or are personally insensitive. It is that the task of active client relationship management can often too easily be crowded out by other activities until some (avoidable) crisis arises which brings it forcibly to the consultant's attention.

ACCOUNT MANAGEMENT

Most business comes from existing clients. The process by which a consultancy engages with existing or past clients – whether or not you are currently conducting any work for them – is how I define 'account management'. The task of account management may be undertaken by consultants alongside other tasks; in some practices, it may be their principal task. In what follows I shall refer to all as 'account managers'.

Account management is an activity that is ongoing irrespective of whether or not the consultancy practice is engaged in a project with a client. The task of the account manager is to maintain the relationship and to see that both client and consultancy extract value from it. For example, the account manager should know of the client's relevant priorities and be in a position to offer relevant consultancy help, should it be required. Expressions of interest arise from both client initiated and consultant developed opportunities. It is the job of the account manager to facilitate both of these.

The allocation of clients to account managers will probably be on the basis of market segmentation.

MARKET SEGMENTATION AND ACCOUNT MANAGEMENT

The need for consultancy services and the manner in which they are sold varies according to segment and therefore it makes sense to allocate clients of similar kinds to the same account manager. The types of segmentation that consultancies use include:
- geographic;
- market sector;
- consultancy service or product.

This segmentation often provides the basis on which the consultancy practice is organised. Thus, a large consultancy may have a London office (geographic segmentation) in which there are specialists marketing IT consultancy services (consultancy service segmentation) to national government bodies (market sector). On the other hand, a sole practitioner may market their services in a specialist area of consultancy across the UK, irrespective of sector.

THE TASK OF THE ACCOUNT MANAGER

An essential process in managing a consultancy firm is illustrated in Exhibit 4.2.

Exhibit 4.2 The role of the account manager

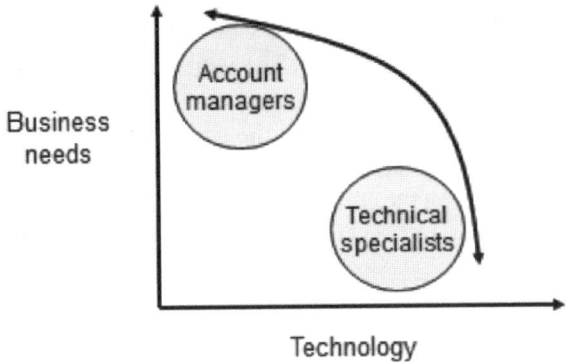

The technological capabilities of a consultancy practice do not readily map on to the business needs of organisations. There needs to be a translation process between the two so that:
- the know-how of consultancy firms can be deployed to best effect within the client organisation;
- the consultancy firm gathers intelligence on the emerging needs of its clients' businesses.

Located in the diagram are technical specialists and account managers. Technical specialists will have a deep understanding of their specialisation and its application, often within a market sector or set of circumstances. In this capacity they will not have the same depth of knowledge of specific client organisations as account managers.

For account managers, the reverse will be true. They will be very close to their client organisations, and have a major responsibility for mediating the connection between business needs and consulting technology.

Performance of the account manager task

The account manager has a major role in promoting the competitiveness of a consultancy firm.

Referring back to Exhibit 4.1, it is worth reflecting where, in a given product-market sector, competitive advantage lies in consultancy. The fact is that the quality of individual consultants is broadly similar (and there is a certain amount of movement between firms). The offerings are also similar, addressing as they do, common predicaments in organisations that are broadly similar. The methodologies, however, to reach the desired outcomes may vary from firm to firm. Moreover, the nature of the relationship, how it is conducted and managed, between individuals in the consultancy firm and those in the client, will also vary.

Treacy and Wiersema suggest that competitive advantage lies in changing what customers value and how it is delivered, then boosting the level of value that customers expect (Harvard Business Review, January-February 1993). They go on to suggest that companies that have taken leadership positions offer superior customer value in one of three value disciplines, whilst meeting or exceeding standards in the other two. The value disciplines they identify are operational excellence, customer intimacy and product leadership. Of these, the latter two are relevant to the job of the account manager.

Customer intimacy is about fitting the offering to the needs of the customer. This is familiar territory to the consultant; every proposal is – at least in theory – the design of a product tailored to the needs of the client. But the perception of 'needs of the client' is all-important; to what extent is it current? So a key task of the account manager is to be acutely aware of – perhaps even anticipate – the particular needs of an organisation and the executives in it for outside support. As one account manager said to me, 'If the first I hear of something significant at one of my clients is in the press, then I'm not doing my job!'

Product leadership concerns continuous production of state-of-the-art products and services. This is of interest to consultancy firms not only in so far as their own activities are concerned, but also in respect of the needs of their clients. The link between consultancy and client is a two-way street in this respect: the consultancy can contribute to the client's thinking, but so too can the client contribute to the consultancy's.

So the account manager has an important strategic role as the conduit between consultancy and client. But there is a further important aspect.

Depth of the relationship

We noted above the importance of the relationship in determining competitive position. It also affects the nature of the work that is undertaken.

Broadly, the work that consultants do for clients can be divided into two kinds:
- Determining the development agenda (also called 'demand side' work);
- Implementing the development agenda (also called 'supply side' work).

The latter follows from the former. Implementation might be, say, of a particular software application for a business's management information system. The need for this, and indeed for the management information system, will be an aspect of the client's development agenda.

Involvement in formulating the development agenda brings you closer to the heart of the business. Consultants engaged in this must of necessity have a close relationship with individual client executives, and have their trust. The corollary is that only those consultants who have this sort of relationship will be allowed by the client to engage in agenda-setting type work.

By contrast, implementation is better defined, and is the continuation of the initiatives on the client agenda. If the task is well defined, it becomes more commoditised, and differentiation is less easy.

So the upshot of this logic is that effective account management is a key differentiator. Which is not so earth shattering – we all prefer to do business with people we like and trust.

MAINTAINING THE CLIENT RELATIONSHIP IN BETWEEN PROJECTS

Although there may be other reasons for networking with a client, the fundamental value derives from the flow of business yielded from investing in the relationship. Think of the relationship as a bridge, while sales are the traffic flowing over it: there is no traffic if there is no bridge; but a bridge is of little value if it carries no traffic.

The value of maintaining the relationship is illustrated in Exhibit 4.3. The Exhibit shows different circumstances in which consultancy and client react to the perception of need.

Exhibit 4.3 The value of maintaining the client relationship

		Does the client recognise the need?	
		No	**Yes**
Do we recognise the need?	**Yes**	Draw to client's attention	Develop a sales discussion
	No	?	Client contacts consultancy

A sales discussion will ensue only if both sides perceive the need, while if neither sees a need, nothing will happen. Account management is particularly pertinent to the other circumstances (depicted in the boxes top right and bottom left) where only one of the parties sees the need.

The cheapest form of selling is when the client asks you for help – they contact you because they see a need for your services (box on bottom right). This they will do only if they are aware of what you do and the key task of the account manager, therefore, in this respect is maintaining awareness. The techniques of doing this include promotional activities applicable to finding new clients, but in addition, the account manager can maintain contact through visits and meetings with client staff. This also helps to fulfil the requirements of the box top left – both in identifying needs and providing the opportunity to find out whether they are apparent and important to the client. Ideally an account manager should be a member of the same business community as their clients.

The state of readiness of a client for a particular project or intervention changes with time. Keeping in contact allows you to check whether a client is now ready for that in which they were not interested a year ago.

FACTORS CONTRIBUTING TO THE QUALITY OF A RELATIONSHIP

For the remainder of this chapter we will be looking at client relationships in the context of a consultancy project.

Every consultancy project starts with a fund of goodwill from the client towards the consultant. There is no particular reason under normal circumstances why this should be exhausted during a project – except by mismanagement! So what a consultant needs to know is the anatomy of client satisfaction (or dissatisfaction), which can be derived from an understanding of the client relationship.

The quality of a client relationship will depend on:
- features of the consultancy practice;
- characteristics of the client;
- the consultancy project being undertaken and its effect on the relationship.

Given an understanding of these, a consultant can plan and manage a client relationship so as to optimise it. The chapter therefore concludes with some suggestions of the skills and activities that will help to create satisfied clients.

FEATURES OF THE CONSULTANCY PRACTICE

One reason that client relationships suffer is that there is a natural conflict between the needs of a consultancy practice and those of its clients. This is illustrated in Exhibit 4.4.

Exhibit 4.4 The different wants of clients and consultancies

Clients want:	Consultancies want:
The most appropriate consultant	To use who's available
Instant attention	To service a number of clients
To pay only for the time spent on the job	To bill as much time as possible
Experienced consultants	To train inexperienced consultants
	To spread experienced people thinly

This conflict becomes focused on the individual consultant, who is subject to demands from several sources. Consultants often have more than one client, each with their own requirements and seeking a level of service as if each was the only client. The consultant also has duties to their own employer and superiors (see Exhibit 4.5).

Exhibit 4.5 Conflicting demands on a consultant

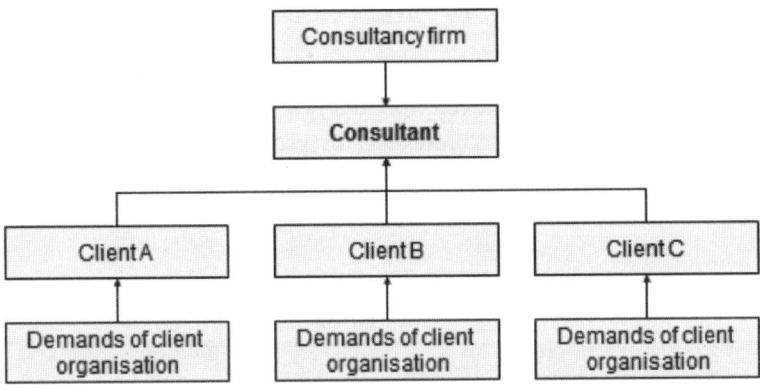

Taken together, these demands may present a consultant with a dilemma; does he look after client A or client B first? Does she carry out the additional work that she knows client C requires, or does she take on the more lucrative work of client D? Consultants will also have their own preferences in terms of the type of work they undertake or clients they deal with, which will also influence the choices they make.

The skill with which consultants can deal with these conflicting demands has a considerable influence over the quality of the client relationship.

CHARACTERISTICS OF THE CLIENT

Not only does the consultant have a responsibility for the quality of a client relationship – the client also has a responsibility. This is not simply policing the services being provided by the consultant – it is active co-operation. The relationship between consultant and client should be a partnership, working together towards the same project goals.

The individual with whom the consultant is dealing will also be subject to demands, as shown in Exhibit 4.5. Sometimes these change and in turn so too do their requirements of the consultant. The consultant must be sufficiently flexible to respond to these changes where necessary.

Another important consideration is how well the client uses consultants. Being an employer does not automatically make someone a good manager.

Similarly, although the client is paying a fee, this does not make them expert at using consultants.

What makes for a good client? One commentator has suggested that 'good' clients bring to the relationship:
- a clear picture of desired results, but not how to achieve them;
- a tough, questioning approach to proposals, demanding to see how a course of action will deliver;
- a recognition of the importance of feedback, so the consultant constantly learns about results, positive or negative, of their interventions;
- an appreciation that it needs time to build a relationship by keeping in touch, taking time to explore the brief and encourage questions, to review feedback and to redesign the project if necessary;
- a sensitivity to the importance of acknowledging a positive contribution: the ability to say 'thank you.'

Helping the client become a good client

In recent years, more attention has been paid to the skills of being a good client. There are recommendations for how best to select and work with consultants to best effect, for example on the UK Institute of Consulting's website which provides a best practice guide. It's useful to think of a consulting project as being a joint venture between consultant and client; and success depends on the performance of both parties.

Not all clients, sadly, exhibit these characteristics, so one of the tasks of consultants is to help their clients to become good clients. After all, if the client has never used consultants before, there is no reason why they should be able to use them well. And, even if they have used them, they may be misguided. So here are three contradictory precepts for consultants to remember in dealing with clients:
- *The client is always wrong.* The popular adage is, of course, 'The customer is always right'. This cannot – must not – be the case in consultancy, where the consultant's role is to take a view independent of the client. You should therefore question the assumptions, objectives and constraints set by clients and ask, 'Are these appropriate?'
- *The client is often right.* Having done the questioning above, the consultant will often come to this conclusion, but there is more to this precept. Sometimes it can be easy for a consultant to develop a mind-set that clients are misguided incompetents, who can do nothing without the help of a consultant. Hence you need to be aware of the strengths of a client's thinking and decisions as well as the weaknesses.
- *Sell them what they need in terms of what they want!* This is well worth repeating. Occasionally there may be a need for confrontation, but the rest of the time – go with the flow. In this sense, dealing with clients is like the art of judo. In judo, skill lies not in opposing

your opponent but in engaging with their energy so that they throw themselves. The art in dealing with clients is to direct their energies so that they move in the desired direction. A technique for doing this is to start in their preferred direction, but to educate them by use of data feedback so they start to look at things differently and move in a more appropriate direction.

THE EFFECT OF THE PROJECT ON THE CLIENT RELATIONSHIP

A consultancy project will affect the client relationship not just in terms of its technical quality, but also through:
- the quality of project;
- performance;
- the quality of the personal relationship between client staff and consultant.

Exhibit 4.6 shows the key elements in each of these.

Exhibit 4.6 Perceptions are all

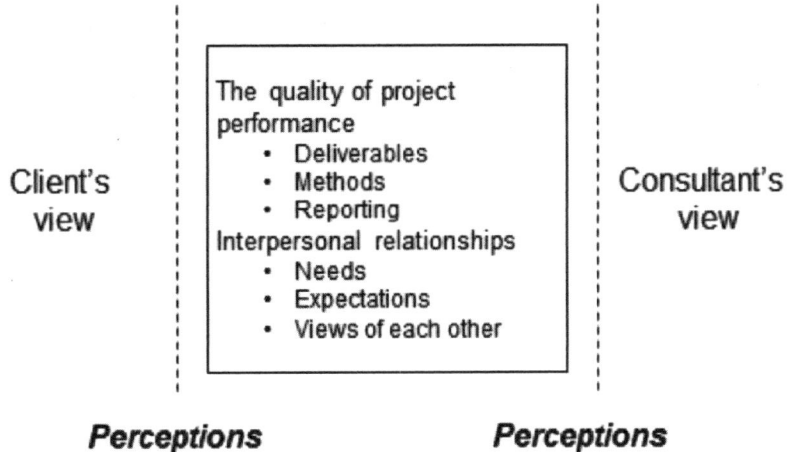

The quality of project performance
It is rarely the technical quality of a project that leads to client dissatisfaction; clients are more interested in ends than means. The key aspect of a project that influences a client relationship is therefore deliverables – what the consultant is to provide to the client. It is for these that the client has engaged and will pay the consultant. The timing of deliverables is also crucial; clients get upset when deliverables are behind schedule.

Methods are the means used to create the deliverables. Problems arise with methods when there is disagreement about the details, or which of the consultant or client was meant to carry out a particular task. Every consultant activity has an impact on the client system. Problems can also occur, therefore, when a project has an unwelcome effect on the client. It is a rare project that does not involve some client participation, so it is important to be clear about:
- who should be involved;
- how they should be involved.

The basis of reporting to the client should also be clear; clients become irritated when they do not feel adequately informed. So this applies to progress reports as well as assignment reports.

The quality of interpersonal relationships

As already mentioned, it is reasonable to assume that at the start of an assignment the consultant team begins with a fund of goodwill from the client. So the aim must be at least to avoid disappointing the client and, preferably, to improve the client's view of the consultants.

As the relationship is between individuals, the quality of the interpersonal relationship between the consultant and the client's staff will have an effect on the total relationship. The important factors are shown in Exhibit 4.6.

The needs of the client must be considered, both in terms of the project and how it is to contribute to the client's personal objectives. Problems occur if a consultant does not discern a client's real needs. Sometimes a client might have a hidden agenda, either as a principal or ancillary objective of the project. (Usually these agendas are political in nature!)

If clients' expectations are not met they will be disappointed and relationships will suffer. You must therefore take care to manage the client's expectations so that they can be met. These expectations relate not only to the project but also to you yourself, for instance, in the way in which you conduct yourself. For example, if you are working on client premises, the client may have firm expectations about:
- what time you should arrive and leave;
- whether you can spend time on the telephone on business other than that to do with the project in hand;
- style of dress;
- your access to people in other departments or at more senior levels;
- the degree of formality in your relationship with client staff.

Infringing these expectations can have just as serious repercussions on the consultant/client relationship as failing to meet the formal terms of reference.

Consequently, many consultants use the period of familiarisation at the start of an assignment to collect data on the 'code of conduct' they are to follow within the client organisation.

In a similar way, you can have quite legitimate expectations of a client. You can reasonably expect the client:
- to be accessible;
- to provide the resources promised;
- to co-operate in the execution of the project;
- to be supportive of the project;
- to tell you of changes of circumstances that may influence the project;
- to discuss any concerns or apprehensions about how the project is proceeding.

Although these are all the responsibilities of the client, you should monitor that they are being provided. If they are not, it is your job, as the expert, to alert the client to any difficulties and advise on how they should be resolved.

How the client and consultant view each other will depend on the other items already mentioned. That relationship will in part be a self-fulfilling prophecy; a client who loses confidence in a consultant will be far more difficult to satisfy.

Occasionally you find that there is conflict between a client and a consultant, or among members of client staff. A good diagnostic rule in analysing conflict is to remember the sequence:
1. Goals.
2. Roles.
3. Procedures.
4. Personal animosity.

What this sequence suggests is that if you do run into conflict, do not assume it is necessarily a matter of personal animosity – there are other possible causes, which are shown in the order of the list above. The easy way to remember the sequence is to imagine two people undertaking a car journey, who are arguing. They will argue if:
1. They have not agreed on where they are going (goals).
2. Although they have agreed where they are going, they have not agreed who is to drive (roles).
3. Although they have agreed on where they are going and who is going to drive, they have not decided the route they are to take (procedures).

If, after agreement on all these points, they are still arguing, then perhaps it can be put down to personal animosity!

PERCEPTIONS ARE ALL

As illustrated in Exhibit 4.6, all the transactions between consultant and client are viewed through their respective perceptions. It is not 'objective reality' which matters but how you each see things.

The client's opinion will be affected by:
1. How they evaluate progress on the project compared with the promises you have made.
2. The impression the client has of the overall professionalism of the practice.

Item (1) above is about communications and expectations. A key job for a consultant in managing client relationships is to reassure the client that the project is proceeding satisfactorily. This means not only communicating progress, but ensuring that the client's expectations accord with those of the consultant. For example, returning to the ICC case study in Chapter 2, John Smith may embark on a project to study alternative methods of producing cutlery, and in so doing, he might choose to discuss the pros and cons of present methods with the operatives at ICC. If, however, the General Manager's view is that there should be no consultation, there is a mismatch of expectations. Keeping the client informed is not just about reporting the past but also managing their expectations for the future.

The impression of the professionalism of a consultancy practice depends on the administrative as well as professional staff. The client comes into contact with switchboard and administrative staff, receptionists, and with accounts people in respect of invoices. Most contacts will be fleeting and will not be face to face, but all will contribute to the client's impression of the practice. Many professional practices have therefore trained all their staff in key aspects of delivering good client care.

MONITORING THE CLIENT RELATIONSHIP

Remember clients will always have a view of the consultant, but whether they tell the consultant of their view is another matter. This is illustrated in Exhibit 4.7.

Note that there is on both sides a threshold of dissatisfaction or satisfaction which must be reached before the client will comment. The consultant's aim must be continuing positive satisfaction, rather than simply assuming that no feedback means that the client is satisfied.

There are two things that the consultant must do to address this:
- Monitor the quality of the client relationship by actively soliciting feedback.

Exhibit 4.7 The client's comments

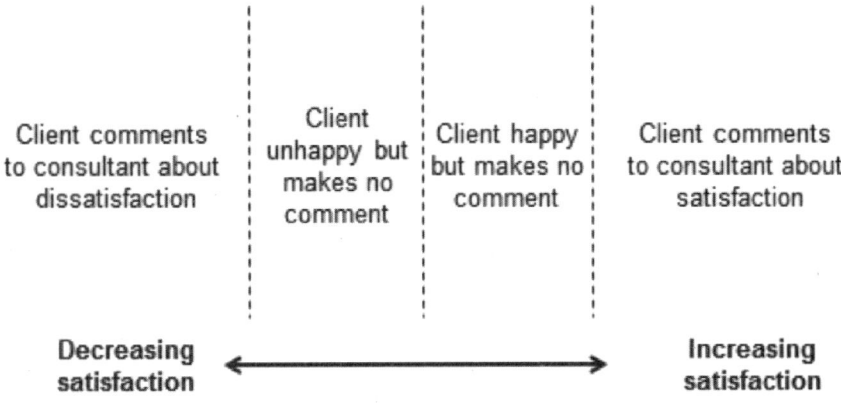

- Adopt good practices in operating consultancy projects, so that the risk of client dissatisfaction is reduced.

Regular progress reviews enable the client to feedback concerns and can be used to manage expectations. Even so, there is a danger that the consultant does not hear what the client is saying; you have to listen carefully to hear softly voiced criticisms.

HANDLING COMPLAINTS

Inevitably from time to time a client may complain about progress or the way a job is being run, or the impact of it on client staff. Do not over-react to complaints – they might not be justified or could be totally unfounded.

Indeed, a complaint is valuable, as it means that the client cares enough to tell you. A complaint enables you to put things right, or to improve service. If the client does not tell you, you cannot put things right.

Here is an effective way of handling a complaint from a client.

1. Thank them for having brought it to your notice and giving you a chance to put it right. (Far better this way than that they should simply get annoyed, leaving the matter unresolved.) Tell them you're sorry they have been upset, but don't apologise for having done something wrong. (You don't even know if it's your fault at this stage, but you can regret their being upset.)
2. Encourage them to give you the full story and note the details. Don't interrupt while the client is giving vent to their feelings and don't argue, however justified you think you may be in doing so – this will only make them more irritated.

3. When you have got all the information, check whether the complaint is founded. Sometimes difficulties arise from misunderstandings and a simple explanation will sort things out. If you cannot deal with the complaint at this meeting, however, explain this and tell the client what you plan to do. In particular, agree when you will get back to them with a response and make sure you do follow up.

A critical test of any provider of goods or services is how they handle complaints. If a complaint is handled professionally and well, it can strengthen rather than weaken the client relationship.

There are sound reasons for this. Complaints usually arise because a client has a problem and when you work with a client to resolve a complaint you are, in effect, engaged in joint problem solving. Joint problem solving strengthens relationships; indeed, it is a mechanism often used in team building programmes. So a capably resolved complaint can strengthen the relationship.

It is important to know when to call for help when dealing with a complaint. This is particularly necessary when a complaint is about you (when you are not in the best position to resolve it) or if the client is seeking some commercial compensation. Sometimes things do go wrong (no consultant is perfect!) but do not compound the mistake by not asking for help when you need it.

CREATING SATISFIED CLIENTS

The comments thus far in this chapter have been somewhat defensive, focusing on how to avoid a poor client relationship. The remainder of this chapter looks at the other side of the coin – how to carry out consultancy projects so that clients are positively satisfied rather than simply 'not dissatisfied.'

This starts with the planning of the project, continues throughout the delivery, and finishes with its completion.

SETTING UP THE PROJECT

Clear and comprehensive terms of reference and terms of business are the foundation of a good client relationship. If you did not sell the assignment, but are operating a project sold by someone else, then you should check that the points below have been covered; if they are not, you must clarify them right at the start of the project:
- The scope of the project;
- The deliverables to the client;
- The method by which you will carry out the project;
- The programme of work involved;

- The resources required, including the support you expect from the client;
- The fees you are charging and when they become payable;
- When the project is to be completed.

You also need to know something of the sponsor, particularly their attitude to the project. What are the payoffs for them if the project is successful – what will they get out of it? How used are they to using outside advice? If a client has not used consultants before, they may need help in using your services to best effect.

PLANNING THE PROJECT

With any project other than the most trivial, it will be necessary to have review or reporting points with the client during its course. Progress reviews should take place at a regular frequency (e.g. once per week or per month) or at milestones – points in the project where a major phase or stage is complete.

Progress reviews can do much to reassure a client that a project is proceeding well and build confidence in the consultant. The converse – not keeping a client informed – can result in their feeling out of control or vulnerable, even if there is no basis for this.

When making your project plan, try to build in some slack so that you have some flexibility to accommodate delays. If your planning is such that any change in circumstances means that you will fail to meet targets, inevitably this will happen.

DURING THE PROJECT

There are several things you can do which will enable you to develop a good client relationship during a project:
- *Build confidence during the early stages.* Every project should start well; after all, you would not have won the contract if the client did not have the confidence that you were the best firm for the job. But during the early stages, even established clients will be checking out the firm's credentials, to see if that first impression was correct. Early in a project it is particularly important, therefore, to build a client's confidence. Being prompt and prepared at all client meetings, perhaps having them more frequently than you might otherwise have, will help; so too will a business-like approach and achieving all the initial targets required on time. One particularly good way of building confidence at

the early stages is the 'quick success' – achieving a result or delivering value beyond that expected.
- *Add value*: The 'quick success' formula will work throughout a project, so try to add value by doing more than the client expects. This does not mean providing free services, but look for opportunities of giving extra benefits from your work or help that may be beyond your brief. The most commercially advantageous to you are those which are valuable to a client but cheap for you to provide. A simple example is giving a client a publication or report from your consultancy practice on a topic of concern to them.
- *Publicise good news*: Make sure the client knows about all the successes you have achieved in your project. This can be done via progress reviews, but also make sure you can bring them up during casual conversations with client staff. If you are really sophisticated you will plan 'sound bites' so that you have a snappy response to the query 'How is it going?' Your sound bite should consist of a 'newsworthy' comment about how the project is progressing. These items can be passed on by client staff. Remember that your client will want to reassure their colleagues that the project is proceeding successfully.
- *Deal with bad news*: If something goes wrong which can be easily remedied without concerning the client, there is no need to bother them. If the client has to be informed, then it is better to do so before the problem becomes a crisis. Ideally you should go to the client with a statement of the problem and how you propose to solve it. Sometimes, however, you may need to work together to resolve the problem. Often clients will put in extra effort to solve the problem or mitigate its effect on their organisation to save their own credibility with their colleagues.

PERSONAL SKILLS OF THE CONSULTANT

There are personal skills that make it easier for consultants to manage client relationships well. These are as follows.

Manage your time effectively
Time is the consultant's stock in trade; it is the commodity that you are selling. Time is also a consultant's scarcest resource, so it must be managed carefully. This requires three important skills:
- Establishing and working to a set of priorities.
- Giving sufficient time to existing commitments.
- Learning to say 'No'. Contrary to popular belief, there are a limited number of hours per day that a consultant can work at optimal

performance. There comes a point when a consultant has to say 'No' to the demands of a practice or the client.

Position yourself correctly

Consultants must position themselves so that they are the equal of the client – at whatever level the client in the organisation is. In particular, the consultant should make clear the right to say 'No' to a client, for example when they have unreasonable fee or time-scale expectations.

Handling conflicting demands

It may not be within the consultant's power to resolve a conflict of demands between a client and the consultancy practice. This is particularly difficult for junior consultants, who could find themselves in a 'no-win' situation – they will upset someone whatever they do. They should seek the help of a more senior consultant – their boss – to resolve it.

When things go wrong, deal with them

Inevitably there will be occasions when things go wrong at either the project or personal level between consultant and client. When this happens, it should be recognised as a problem and dealt with as such. It is the way a consultant deals with problems which is a key test of how good they are at managing the client relationship. Young consultants are frequently reluctant to admit to mistakes that they cannot deal with; far better to admit them, however, before they turn into crises.

Don't knock anybody

It is rarely to a consultant's credit to criticise their colleagues, their clients or their competitors to their client. Where a client has a justifiable complaint about a consultant colleague, the consultant should acknowledge and deal with it rather than denigrating the colleague.

Be attentive

A lot of effort goes into wooing the client to win their business. Once the business has been secured, the client will still expect attentive service. In practice this means that the consultants must be accessible to their clients and give them prompt attention. Equally, the consultant must be able to avoid the 'time wasters' without losing them as clients.

THE END OF THE PROJECT

I am told that in at least one European country there is the phrase, 'To say goodbye like an Englishman,' which means to go without saying goodbye!

The best source of further work and referrals to new clients is past clients, and so every project should be concluded with this in mind.

The project should be signed off from both sides – the consultancy's and the client's. There should be a clear agreement on the successful completion of the project and perhaps an exchange of letters confirming the client's satisfaction. And astute consultants will make sure that warm letters of praise from clients are passed on to their own superiors.

5
PRODUCT DEFINITION AND MARKETING IN CONSULTANCY

Consultancy activities are frequently referred to as services but herein we will be referring to them as *products*. Consultancy products are the means by which value is added to the client and so we start with the notion of product definition.

Product definition and market definition go hand in hand, so this chapter continues with some thoughts about marketing consultancy products. In this text, marketing relates to clients in general, while selling is to specific clients.

Ralph Waldo Emerson wrote, 'If a man... make a better mouse-trap than his neighbour, tho' he build his house in the woods, the world will make a beaten path to his door.' But your efforts will avail you naught if the world doesn't recognise the need for a mousetrap, or doesn't know you've built a better one, or has no idea where your door is.

Exhibit 5.1 Business development in a consultancy firm

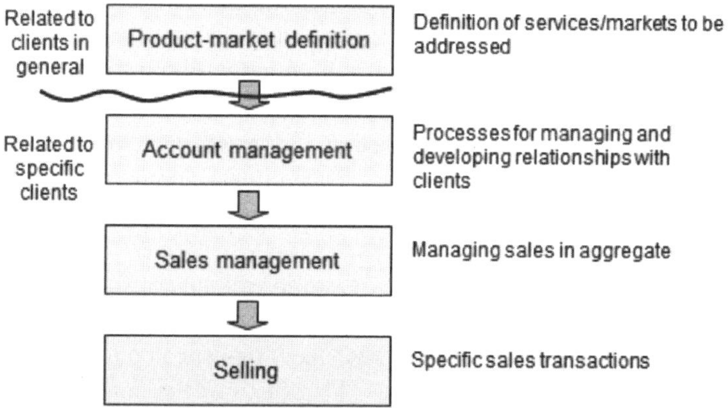

Related to clients in general	Product-market definition	Definition of services/markets to be addressed
Related to specific clients	Account management	Processes for managing and developing relationships with clients
	Sales management	Managing sales in aggregate
	Selling	Specific sales transactions

So what is the consultancy 'mousetrap' (product) and how can you market and sell it? These topics are addressed using the model shown in Exhibit 5.1. This shows the hierarchy of matters to be considered.
- *Product-market definition* is the foundation of the business.
- *Account management* describes how the consultancy relates to its clients. Account management is ongoing, whether or not the consultancy is currently doing work for that client.
- *Sales management* is about managing the sales process and sales in aggregate whereas, by contrast...
- *Selling* is about conducting a single sales transaction.

PRODUCT-MARKET DEFINITION

The basic activities involved in consultancy (the topics covered in this book) vary very little. Similarly consultancy products offer the same old wine in new bottles. Skills in issue analysis, data collection, diagnosis and creating change within a client environment, will be common to many consultancy offerings. In the same way that a cabinet maker may change his designs to suit current fashion but continue to use the same skills, management consultants focus their perennial skills on organisational matters of current concern – for example, on cost reduction in a recession, on growth strategies in a boom.

Product definition in consultancy is best described as the packaging of experience (represented by both knowhow and data) which is then communicated through marketing and selling. Experience may be imported with a new recruit, or it may derive from experience in carrying out consultancy projects for clients; either way, if it is to be sold, it has then to be packaged into a consultancy service – something that can be replicated.

Wherever it is positioned, the consultancy service has to be communicable. In the same way that a cabinet maker would find it easier to describe his craft in terms of the products he makes, so too consultants need to describe their services in terms of the processes used and the benefits arising from them. For example, a consultancy employed an expert in knowledge engineering for the first time – the only specialist of his kind within the firm. He had no previous experience of consultancy and the consultancy was not quite clear what he had on offer. The results were that his specialist experience was never sold because it had not been packaged as a communicable offering.

There are other similarities between the consultant and the cabinet maker. The job that the cabinet maker does, for example, depends on the customer's specification. Similarly, the job done by the consultant consists of harnessing their skills to meet the requirements of the terms of reference as agreed. A difference, however, is that whereas the cabinet maker can point to other items of furniture he may have created, it is less easy for the consultant to do so because the consulting product is intangible. This is commonly dealt with by using references from previous clients or citing previous experiences, which can refer to the activities involved and results achieved.

Even when a consultancy has had some success in carrying out projects in a particular area, there is some merit in packaging this experience. For example, if a consultancy had developed an approach that helped employers to reduce levels of absenteeism by half, this would be of great interest to large organisations. Few buyers, however, would have sufficient confidence to commission a consultancy project simply because the consultants asserted this was possible; they would want to know how these results were achieved and perhaps speak with other clients for whom the consultants had done a similar job in the past. All these are steps that serve to reduce the buyer's sense of risk and increase their confidence.

Ultimately, all that a client gets when they commission a consultancy project is a promise. Packaging a consultancy product increases the client's confidence that the promise can be kept.

A packaged consultancy product consists of:
- *A name*. At best, this can become a brand (e.g. 'The X job evaluation system') or at the least make reference to it simple (e.g. 'activity based costing').
- An *explanation* of its purpose and the methodology used in carrying it out.
- Descriptions of *situations* in which it might be of use and the benefits of doing so.
- Information on *previous applications* of the technique and the benefits obtained.

Often a consultancy will publish a brochure describing the product or at least show it as a web page; in this case, to the above list would be added information to meet the criteria set out in the section on 'Marketing objectives' below. Finally, if consultancy salespeople are to promote the product, they will need 'golden nuggets': stories illustrating the benefits of introducing the consultancy product (useful for clients to tell their colleagues), together with some indication of the likely costs of consultancy help.

I have often found it useful to test out new product concepts with friendly clients. Although not necessarily prospective purchasers of the product, they can be an invaluable source of feedback from a client's point of view.

There are some who, with some justification, claim that consultancy is a fashion business. The list of fashionable products from the past is extensive: process re-engineering, quality circles, overhead value analysis, management by objectives, total quality management, were all popular in their time. And all have delivered value to their users, but may now be out of fashion. There is therefore a need for consultancies – as with any other business – to maintain a flow of new products to meet the needs of their customers. Fashion may not be rational; but ignoring fashion in consultancy is like telling a couturier that the only purpose of clothing is to keep the rain off! And, to be fair, the delivery of 'old fashioned' products can be improved with increasing experience, and then repackaged and relaunched.

JOINT VENTURES AND STRATEGIC ALLIANCES

Moving from fashion to food as an analogy, in many respects, consultancy product development has characteristics similar to cookery. A skilled chef, working from a small range of ingredients, can create a wide variety of appealing dishes. In a similar way, consultants put together capabilities to create offerings attractive to clients.

In Chapter 1, we saw that consultants associate for this purpose, but often the capabilities required do not lie within a single firm of consultants and so they engage in joint ventures. 'Capabilities' in this context may not simply mean technical abilities – it might mean access to a market, or a depth of resource. For example, in entering a foreign market a consultancy might seek a joint venture partner.

Although it may not be involved in a strategic alliance, a large consultancy will need to become accustomed to forming consortia to bid for major projects. Resources required for projects in these circumstances will be drawn from subcontractors and joint ventures, working within a framework of the consultancy's own methodologies.

Having defined the consultancy product, the firm now needs to decide how best to project it to its target market sectors.

BRANDING IN CONSULTANCY

Within any business, you need to decide what you want to be famous for. Branding is the aggregation of these attributes.

Exhibit 5.2 shows how consultancy offerings relate to the type of branding.

At one end of the spectrum in Exhibit 5.2 the offering is shown as being about services. These are methodologies that are pre-defined, although their application may be tailored to the needs of a client. A good example is a proprietary job evaluation system, whose principles of operation and method of introduction to a business will be standardised, although the details will be varied according to each client's requirements. Such an offering is solution related – i.e. the problem has already been defined. Under these circumstances, the product should be branded – e.g. the XYZ job evaluation system.

Exhibit 5.2 The branding of consultancy offerings

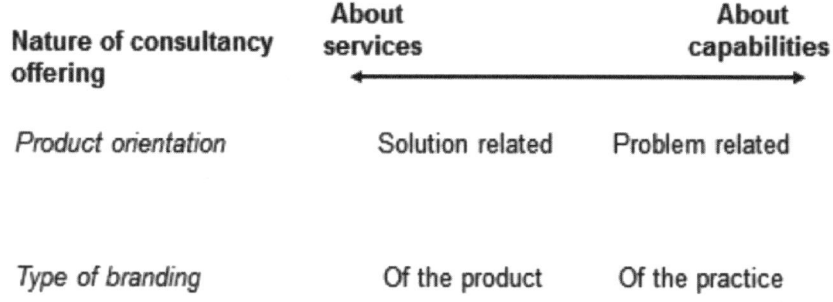

At the other end of the spectrum, the offering is shown as being about capabilities. Practices in this position may offer an embracing methodology for working with clients in dealing with problems of a particular type. This is an approach to conducting projects rather than being related to a particular area of service. In these circumstances, Exhibit 5.2 suggests that the practice should be branded.

The difference between product and practice branding can be illustrated by an example from retail. Imagine that your aunt who lives in London has been invited to a special event for which she needs a new outfit. She might say, 'I've no idea what to wear; I'll go along to Harrods to see if they have any ideas.' This is the equivalent of practice branding; she is going to Harrods because of its reputation, but with no specific purchase in mind.

Alternatively, she might say, 'I think I need a beige dress in classic style – I'll visit Oxford Street to see if I can find one.' This case is equivalent to product branding – she knows what she wants, and has to find someone to provide it.

In the context of consultancy, a firm may promote itself as 'specialists in managing change'. They have not said what kind of change they are involved in, and so are seeking to brand their practice. By contrast, another consultancy firm may offer a service called 'Office Move', dealing with all aspects of helping a business relocate. Businesses will be more attracted to 'Office Move' if they have decided that relocation is what is required.

There is some strategic advantage in branding the firm rather than the service. The prospective client may not be able to see the link between the service and the problem with which they are confronted (although the consultancy's promotional literature will seek to make this clear). Unless the client can be persuaded to see the service as addressing the problem, then they may reject the consultancies offering these, instead preferring to go straight to those practices that specialise in the sort of problems confronting them. The providers of solutions are like – say – a Chinese restaurant: if you want Chinese food, the ideal place to go, but not otherwise. A further advantage for the firm branded as dealing with problems is that they will usually have to start with some diagnosis. This positions them well for follow-on work in creating and implementing solutions to the problems, as well as extending the size of their market. By contrast, the client will have done much of the diagnosis for those offering solutions. For example, if approaching a recruitment consultant, a client will have already diagnosed the need for a recruit.

Given the advantages for the branded firm, consultancy firms will often have the strategic aim of moving from product branding to practice branding. The risk for those who are the providers of solutions only in doing this is that the results of their studies will always be the same – whatever the starting conditions, the same solution is prescribed. Like Henry Ford, they offer 'any colour, as long as it's black'.

MARKETING CONSULTANCY

A simple distinction between marketing and selling consultancy services is that in selling you have a specific client in view; by contrast, marketing is to a specific sector – i.e. many prospective clients. Note that I have taken a limited definition of marketing as essentially the promotion of a consultancy firm and its services. Marketing purists would no doubt argue for a broader definition, emphasising the need for the whole business to be marketing oriented. Consultancy, however, is by nature a peculiarly market oriented business. Most people of any seniority in a firm – if not most consultants – have daily contact with their customers; few businesses outside the professions can boast as much contact. Moreover, every professional is called on to promote, if not sell, their firm's services, which again requires a strong market orientation.

The aim of marketing is to:
- generate a demand for and raise awareness of a consultancy product;
- help to generate or identify good prospects;
- position the practice as a provider of (the defined) consultancy services.

Marketing in a consultancy business therefore consists largely of promotional activities. There may be, of course, professional restrictions on the methods by which consultants may promote themselves; for example, many years ago advertising was forbidden by some professional associations. However, over recent years the restrictions seem to have become far fewer..

MARKETING OBJECTIVES

There are five criteria that have to be satisfied before a client will open a dialogue on working together with a consultant. They are:

1. The client has to recognise that a problem exists.
2. The client must believe that the problem is sufficiently important to merit attention.
3. The client must believe that the problem can be resolved.
4. The client must decide that outside help is required to resolve the problem.
5. The client must decide that your practice is worth considering for this work.

Thereafter there will be further hurdles for the consultancy to surmount before receiving an invitation to tender, which must be dealt with as part of the sales process.

The objectives of marketing should be to help to see that these criteria are satisfied. The consultancy which is attempting to market a new service may have to start at stage 1. At the other extreme, stages 1 to 4 may have been completed by the client without any prompting from a consultancy practice; it merely remains for the client to select a consultancy to work on the project. This is the case, for example, where a consultancy receives an invitation to tender from a client. (In the public sector there may be regulations requiring invitations to tender for projects above a certain value to be publicised so that anyone can respond.)

Set out below are the activities you can undertake that will help to satisfy these criteria.

The client has to recognise that a problem exists: To go to a client with the offer of a service to solve a problem that they do not recognise as such stands as much chance of success as a plumber who wants to repair your central heating when nothing is wrong. Clients recognise problems when:

- There is a problem or opportunity where previously none was thought to exist. Often these arise from change in the environment, for example:
  - a social trend – e.g. concern with corporate social responsibility;
  - new business regulations;
  - a disruptive technological innovation;
  - a government initiative.

  The job of the account manager or salesperson in these circumstances is to draw the attention of the client to the problem.
- The problem is generally recognised, but the client did not know it occurred in their organisation. This is when data feedback is often used by consultants – for example a general survey of some feature of a business sector so that clients can compare the performance of their own organisation with those of others. A contemporary example is in cyber security, where there is a high possibility of hacking by unfriendly individuals into an organisation's confidential data.

The client has to believe that the problem is important: Organisations are rife with problems. Many of the problems are liveable with or they eventually go away. No organisation can afford to be problem free – there is a point of diminishing returns below which it is not worth eliminating a problem. The way the consultancy markets in this respect is to show how the prospective returns are higher than the client originally thought.

Sometimes consultancies undertake a free survey to see whether the problem merits attention and, if so, what the likely return will be. For example, a consultancy that specialises in managing utility consumption (electricity, water, etc.) might see whether any worthwhile reduction in consumption could be achieved by using their own special techniques.

The client must believe that the problem can be resolved: In organisations, most people have plenty to do so do not want to waste their time attempting to resolve insoluble problems.

The marketing task here is confidence building. If someone comes to you and says 'I have a piece of kit which, attached to your car, will double your mileage per litre of petrol,' you might be sceptical. If you were to be assured by other users whose opinions you trusted that this was the case, then you might buy the kit. A reputation for success helps enormously.

The client must want outside help: Despite consultants perhaps wishing otherwise, organisations normally expect to be able to solve their problems for themselves! Sometimes competition for an assignment therefore arises from the client's own staff rather than another consultancy. Exhibit 5.3 sets out some benefits of each.

Exhibit 5.3 Relative benefits of using outside consultants and internal staff

Benefits of outside consultants	**Benefits of internal staff**
Objective	Know the internal politics
Provide an additional resource	Have to be paid anyhow
Experienced at dealing with this type of project	Experienced at dealing with this organisation
Can change consultant personnel if client not satisfied	High incentive to please this client (employer!)

Of course these are not exclusive benefits. A consultancy may know a long-established client very well; alternatively, an internal member of staff may be very expert at dealing with the type of problem to be resolved.

The job of consultants in marketing themselves at this point is to show how well equipped they are to address this type of problem, which is the purpose of promotional material. (Clients may well expect consultants to support the development of the capability of the client's own staff as part of the project).

The client must seek your help: Clients will seek your help only if they know it is available. The purpose of marketing activity is to maintain awareness of your services among key people through promotional activities.

WHO TO MARKET TO

Research has shown that consultants get only 10-20% of their work directly through sales promotion to new clients; the remainder comes from past clients and referrals. Promotion is vital, however, as a flow of new clients is required to maintain a consultancy business, let alone grow it. This is because there is usually some client loss – a client may go out of business, or choose to use a competitor, or may even have no problems left you can help with! And with lively activity in mergers and acquisitions, it's entirely possible that they may cease to exist. So sales promotion is directed at prospective users of a consultancy's services.

Referrals come from connectors. Referrals can be introductions or leads, leads being introductions to prospective clients who have an immediate need for your services. Some professions are very accustomed to using connectors; for example, at a local level accountants cultivate bankers to get introductions to the bankers' clients, and there can be a flow in the other direction. Connectors for consultants depend on the nature of the specialisation. Typically, referrals come from:
- existing or past clients, or individuals with whom you have done business who have moved to new organisations;
- personal contacts;
- other consultancies (where not in competition);
- professional associations;
- other professional advisers.

In marketing to these, a consultancy aims to create a network. A strong network is necessary for all consultancies, whether a sole practitioner or a firm of thousands of professionals.

Often newcomers to consultancy underestimate the value of a good network. Junior consultants forget that they should cultivate their own networks as much as their more senior colleagues. In particular, they are well positioned to identify and network with rising stars in the client organisations with which they have worked.

Some two-thirds or more of a consultancy's business comes directly from past clients, and so they are obvious targets for receiving promotional material for new services. The advantages for a client in using the same consultancy for more than one project are that:
- they will have established an effective *modus operandi* for working together;

- the client will be confident in the consultancy;
- the consultancy will have learned about the client and the client's business.

Sometimes these factors will outweigh other considerations; once (when working as a sole practitioner) a client said to me of a new piece of work he had asked me to do, 'I realise that this is not at the centre of your expertise, but I think you can do a good job for us. You know us and we know you, which is far more important.' (Which is also very gratifying, provided you can do the job!)

So existing clients should be a fruitful source of new business, by selling them additional services.

In large consultancies this presents a further need for marketing; no single individual can be in contact with all clients and know all the consultancy's services. There will be consultants who have account management responsibilities who themselves are specialists. They need to be informed of the other services the consultancy has on offer, and so the process of internal marketing has to be conducted in large practices. Account managers are internal connectors to the consultancy's clients, and so the provider of a specialist skill needs to promote it to these connectors as much as externally. Indeed, some commentators have estimated that in a large consultancy as much effort goes into internal marketing as external.

There remains the question of who to target as new clients. A useful technique here is to profile existing purchasers of your services and identify other organisations that have similar characteristics. These might be defined in terms of size, business sector, current circumstances or predicaments and so on.

You then need to find a point of entry to the new prospective client. Again, you need to know who the typical purchasers of your services might be and then direct your promotional activities towards them.

This is not necessarily a sure-fire method, however. Some years ago, a colleague remarked that she had been in contact with a target client organisation and been told that there was no need for our services. In fact, our firm was already working extensively with this client! Two lessons emerge:
- 'No' is not necessarily a final answer.
- Make sure you organise your selling so that you are not wasting promotional effort trying to win current clients!

PROMOTIONAL ACTIVITIES

Promotional activities can relate to the practice, the service, or the individual consultant.

Practices promote themselves through advertising and sponsorship. Some larger ones have even gone to the considerable expense of using TV advertising. The aim here is to promote general capability rather than a specific service. This is particularly appropriate for large practices with a wide range of services. Some make use of promotional videos, which they can show to prospective new clients, again with the aim of promoting the strength of the practice. This is corporate advertising – something that large organisations in other sectors have practised for years.

The methods by which practices promote their services among prospective and existing clients are:
- brochures and other promotional publications;
- house magazines or journals;
- articles in newspapers and magazines;
- carrying out, or sponsoring, research into a topic of interest, and making this available as a report;
- conferences, seminars, meetings, workshops, etc;
- entertainment – lunches, attendance at sporting occasions or other events.

The ways in which individuals in practices promote their services – or those of the practice – are:
- writing articles for newspapers and other periodicals or publishing books;
- use of social media – e.g. writing blogs;
- appearances on TV or radio;
- membership of national or local bodies – professional associations, business or other societies.

The combination of these activities with networking can enable an individual consultant to become part of the client community they serve. It can then be perfectly natural for organisations to turn to this particular consultant and their firm for help when needed.

A website is also an essential marketing tool. One of the values of a website is that it can be found by prospective clients who are looking for services that the consultancy can offer. The chances of contacting a client on the day they have a need for your services is low; but a client who might need your services may well find your website. So as well as providing up to date information about the consultancy practice and its services, its presence on suitable search engines can generate sales enquiries. It allows prospective clients an easy way of getting information about your business.

These methods used to promote individuals and services can also be used to promote the practice as a whole.

6

THE CONSULTANCY SALES PROCESS

If you are sick and want treatment, you must go to a doctor. If you run a company, you are required to have an auditor. If you have legal problems, you need to consult a lawyer. Nobody has to have a management consultant. Consultants must therefore sell their services actively if they are to survive.

Simple arithmetic shows the commercial imperative to sell in a consultancy practice. Assume you have a medium sized firm with 25 consultants with a basic pay, on average, of £40,000 p.a. Assume that fully absorbed on-costs and overheads are as much again as their salaries. The annual expenses of that consultancy will be £2 million. The fee income has to be £8,000 per working day just to cover costs. Sales of consultancy work obviously have to equal this if the firm is to break even.

It is a fortunate business that can generate sales at this level without any selling effort. Selling has to be active. If professionals are to be able to pursue their calling, there has to be an economic base sufficient to support them. The same applies to internal consultants. Although they may be 'free of charge', they receive a salary and incur other costs; they too have to justify their existence commercially.

How to manage selling is an issue for a practice with any more than a few professionals in it. There has to be some co-ordination through an organisation structure, systems and procedures. Key to managing selling is recognising that time is a consultant's stock in trade. If selling can be done more efficiently, hence requiring less time, a consultancy has a competitive advantage.

A simple example illustrates this. Imagine that a one-man consultancy practice has 180 days available for work each year, after allocating time to holidays, continuing professional development and administration. The consultant has set a revenue target of £75,000 for the year. If his sales ratio is 50 per cent, this means that he has to spend one day selling to generate two days' work. (This selling time would include pursuing unsuccessful prospects, as well as successful sales.) This means that he has to spend 60 days selling to generate 120 days' work. To reach his revenue target, his fee rate has to be (£75,000/120 =) £625 per day. If, however, he is a more successful salesman with a sales ratio of 20 per cent, he would generate five days of sales for each day spent selling. In his year of 180 days, therefore, he would spend 30 days selling and 150 days earning fees. He would therefore need to charge only £500 per day to reach his target revenue. Alternatively, were he to charge the same as he would need to if he were less effective (i.e. £625 per day), his annual income would be £93,750 or 25 per cent more.

The reason, therefore, for being concerned with selling performance is to optimise this sales ratio.

THE CONSULTANCY SALES PROCESS

Product market definition was dealt with in Chapter 5; but three other elements shown in Exhibit 5.1 (account development, sales management and selling) relate to selling to specific clients.

Each of these depends on an understanding of the tasks involved in selling consultancy – the consultancy sales process.

Exhibit 6.1 The consultancy sales process

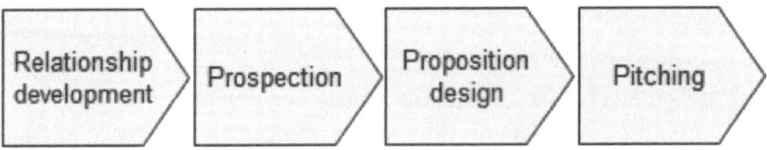

The overall consultancy sales process is illustrated in Exhibit 6.1. Although a continuum of activity, it can be broken down into four main steps:

1. *Relationship development*: At the outset, a consultancy firm and prospective client may have no contact history or knowledge of each other. A relationship between consultancy and client has to be established before any sale can be developed.
2. *Prospection*: In the same way that gold prospectors pan for valuable nuggets, the next stage of the sales process is to identify opportunities for consultancy and client to work together.
3. *Developing the proposition*: Having found an area in which you might work together, the next step is to refine exactly what is going to be done. The consultancy may have a standard approach, but even in these cases, it must be tailored to meet the client's specific needs.

4. *Pitching for the sale*: Having developed the proposition, it must be put over to the client in a compelling way. (And it may be that at this stage, having heard what the consultancy is proposing, the client rethinks what they want and you return to stage 3).

Each of these is described in the following sections together with the critical factors influencing the performance of each.

RELATIONSHIP DEVELOPMENT

The sales processes involved in developing relationships with new and existing clients are known as *hunting* and *farming* respectively.

Traditionally, a hunter goes out to find his quarry – departing from his home territory to wherever his quarry might be found. In like manner, the hunter-salesperson goes out beyond the existing client base to find new clients. By contrast, the farmer stays on his homeland and uses that to produce the food required; the farmer-salesperson produces new sales from an existing client base.

Both hunting and farming are necessary, but – like their rural analogies – sales people often have a preference and aptitude for one rather than the other.

The hunting process starts with *suspects* – those organisations that might need your consultancy services. If yours is a large consultancy, then all organisations might be suspects for the full range of your services. (Size of client organisation is not necessarily a limit; I have worked for one of the largest corporations in the world in the same year that I also worked for an organisation of only six people.) Such a large number of suspects is not helpful, and so it is best to categorise them according to consultancy product.

The number of suspects might also be reduced by market segmentation e.g. geography or industrial sector.

From this long list of suspects you would select a shorter list of organisations to approach – i.e. *prospects*. These might be selected against criteria such as:
- *A need for your service*. This might be general (e.g. organisations are usually interested in worthwhile ideas for increasing performance) or event driven (e.g. a company that has just made a new acquisition, or expanded into a new market).
- *Ease of access*. For example, you might choose to avoid companies that you know have a good relationship with one of your competitors who can supply the same consultancy services that you are trying to sell.

The next stage is to warm up the prospect so that they will agree to a meeting. This is a limited objective – i.e. the approach is not to get the prospect to buy, but to secure the meeting – or to disqualify the organisation as a prospect (see 'Qualification' in Chapter 7). The purpose of the meeting is to start building a relationship, and initiate the prospection process.

Exhibit 6.2 shows a model of hunting as a sort of target: the closer to the bull's-eye, the better the chances of success.

Exhibit 6.2 Developing relationships with new clients

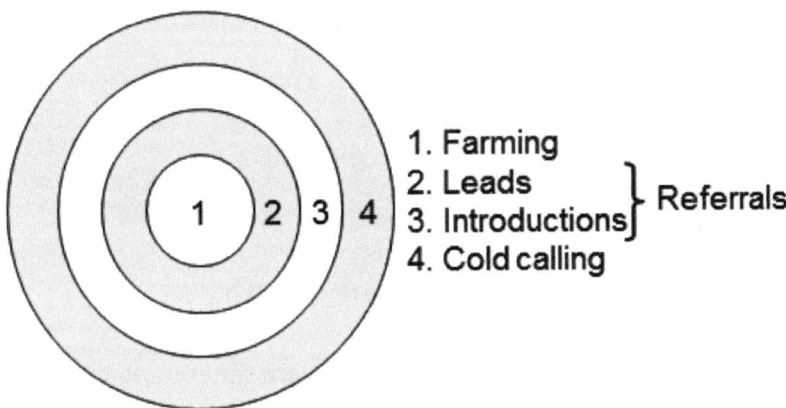

At the centre is shown farming; the link between hunting and farming is described below.

Moving out from the bull's-eye are shown leads and introductions. Both are kinds of referral via a connector. An introduction is to a client who might need your consultancy services. A lead is more than an introduction, in that the connector has seen an immediate requirement for the type of consultancy that you might offer.

Cold calling is the least fruitful of hunting activities as, in the words of one salesperson, 'You have to kiss a lot of frogs before you find a prince'. Cold calling with a telephone call out of the blue is least likely to work; 'warming up' clients beforehand is important so that they will be more receptive to that telephone call when it does come.

Farming is about developing relationships with existing clients. Exhibit 6.3 illustrates how this can be done.

'Point of entry' refers to a part of the organisation that may buy your services. A small organisation may have only one purchaser of consultancy, but large ones have many. You may therefore seek new points of entry to existing clients. Similarly, you may try to sell services other than those being purchased already.

The core activity lies in the bottom left hand quadrant of the figure. You need first to ensure that existing clients continue to use your practice to supply services as in the past. For example, a consultant in logistics would want to secure all consultancy work in this area from an existing client. If the client

Exhibit 6.3 Developing relationships with existing clients

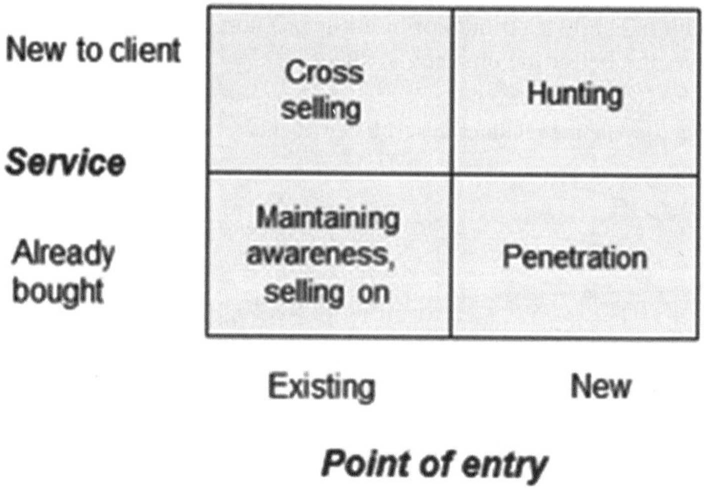

	Existing	New
Service – New to client	Cross selling	Hunting
Service – Already bought	Maintaining awareness, selling on	Penetration

Point of entry

gave a project to a competitor, this would place the consultant's existing business under threat. So you have to nurture clients so that your firm is the one that comes to mind when new opportunities arise for services that they have used in the past. This is about maintaining awareness.

Selling new services to an existing point of entry is called cross selling; establishing new points of entry with an existing client is penetration.

If the salesperson is seeking to sell new services to a new point of entry, this is an activity similar to hunting, when you can get warm leads and introductions from one part of the organisation to another.

EXTRINSIC AND INTRINSIC SELLING

Imagine that you are moving house and you have a solicitor who is carrying out the conveyancing for you. At your final meeting with her, you remark that you plan to install a new central heating system in your house before you move in. Your solicitor then says, 'Oh, I can do that for you – I practise plumbing as well as law.'

Now, it may be that your solicitor is the best and cheapest plumber to do this job, but you would need some convincing to accept her in this role. If she was to persuade you to consider her services, she would have to engage in *extrinsic selling*.

Extrinsic selling legitimises the seller as a provider of a product or service. In the example above, the solicitor has to convince you that she is indeed a bona fide plumber before you would even start to discuss the work that you need doing.

So extrinsic selling is persuading the prospective client that your consultancy practice is worth doing business with in the first place. By contrast *intrinsic selling* is persuading the client of the merit of a specific proposition. Intrinsic selling will not be successful unless the extrinsic sales process has been completed, but completing the extrinsic sales process does not imply success in completing the intrinsic one. Continuing the example above, even if your solicitor does convince you that she can install your new heating system, you might seek quotations from other plumbers to make sure that her quotation is competitive and, if it isn't, you would choose another. Likewise, you will not deal with – say –an insurance broker unless you are convinced that they can provide you with the service you want (the extrinsic process). On the other hand, you will not necessarily accept every suggestion they make concerning the insurance policies you might invest in (the intrinsic process).

So every sale consists of these two stages of extrinsic followed by intrinsic selling. Given the importance of managing time effectively in selling, then the less time that has to be spent on extrinsic selling, the more that can be spent on the intrinsic stage – making specific sales.

Marketing and promotion help the extrinsic sales process by developing a brand. The value of a brand is that it helps with extrinsic selling. If your consultancy practice is well known for its skill in introducing production control systems, say, less effort is required to legitimise your consultancy offering in this area to a specific client. On the other hand, the same consultancy would have greater difficulty in selling projects in – say – marketing, unless it was equally well known in its target market for this.

Note that in hunting, there has to be considerable extrinsic selling activity before you can engage in intrinsic selling. This is in marked contrast to the farming selling process because less effort is required in selling extrinsically to existing clients – they have already accepted your *bona fides* as a consultant. It is for this reason that consultants sell mainly to their existing client base. From the client's point of view too, there are advantages in dealing with the same consultant. It takes time to educate a consultant into the ways of a client's business. Dealing with a consultant used in the past avoids this time and cost.

It is worth noting that some extrinsic selling is required when seeking to sell new products or services to existing clients. This is vividly exemplified by IT hardware suppliers when they started to offer consultancy services. Faced with increasing competition and diminishing margins in their traditional markets, they enlarged their services to include consultancy. This presented a challenge to their sales forces. Say the names of any hardware supplier to a client and they would think of them as a hardware supplier; there was no need to legitimise them as such. When it came to their services as consultants, however, salespeople had for the first time to engage much more in extrinsic selling to persuade their clients to accept them as bona fide consultants. This is now being replicated in many other technology industries (e.g. telecoms) as they try to differentiate their services by capitalising on their knowhow.

PROSPECTION

Exhibit 6.4 shows the steps in the prospection process. It involves mainly intrinsic selling if the consultancy practice is already legitimised as a provider of consultancy services, and a relationship has been formed with the prospective client. If this is not the case, extrinsic selling is needed to position the consultancy and its offerings.

Exhibit 6.4 Steps in the prospection process: EDIT

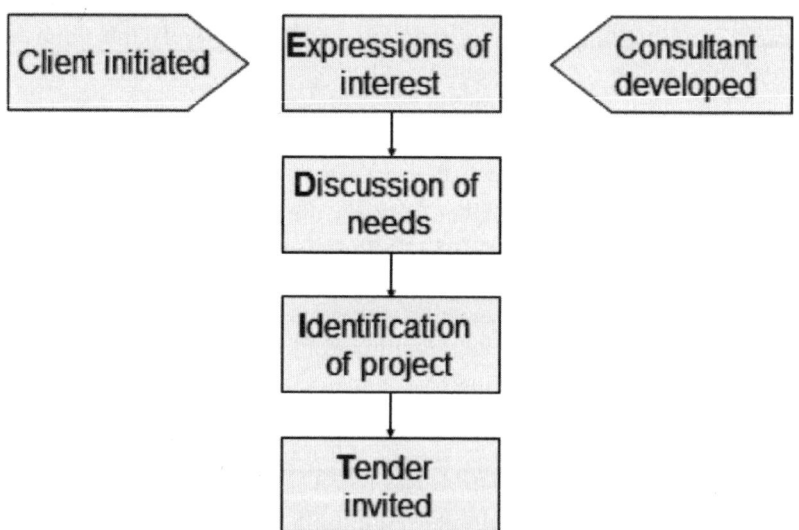

The easiest form of selling is where a client contacts you with a consultancy opportunity and asks for help. Clients will initiate contact only if they have some idea of the services and capabilities you have on offer, so raising and maintaining prospective clients' awareness of them is important. This is the task of promotional marketing, which is dealt with in Chapter 5. These opportunities are not necessarily exclusive; a consulting firm may be on the tender list for a particular organisation and therefore receive invitations to tender as a matter of course.

The other (and more usual) method of prospection shown in Exhibit 6.4 is for the consultancy to be proactive by taking the initiative to develop sales. Strictly speaking, it should not be an option – a consultancy should be continually looking for opportunities to help their clients. An opportunity can be developed by the consultancy when:

- there is an event of some significance for the client (e.g. an announcement of business expansion, the loss of a key customer);
- there is a major change in the client's market sector – e.g. new regulatory or environmental restrictions;
- you have a new service that could be of interest to the client;
- there is significant development among the client's competitors, which could result in a loss of competitive position;
- you have a strong view about an operational or strategic aspect of the client's business, and want to draw the client's attention to this.

On this last point it is worth emphasising that I do believe that consultants can be advocates. It is in our interests to have successful clients – a consultancy firm will not flourish if its clients go out of business. If therefore as a consultant you can see an opportunity for a client to develop their business performance, then you should make representations to them about it.

Indeed, the account management process in some practices has been formalised in respect of creating opportunities, rather than leaving it to happenstance. Someone in the consultancy account team will have the responsibility for looking ahead at the future needs of the client and making plans for how these are to be met, where appropriate, by providing consultancy support.

The 'EDIT' process illustrated in Exhibit 6.4 shows the progress towards an invitation to tender (ITT) or request for proposal (RFP). The four stages can be thought of as a funnel, as each does not automatically lead to the next. For example:
- Although the prospect may be interested, there is no immediate need for any activity in this area.
- Discussion of needs shows that no external support is required.
- The identification of the project shows that it lies outside the capabilities of your practice.

Only once these hurdles have been surmounted will you receive an invitation to tender.

DEVELOPING THE PROPOSITION

Consultancy is one of the least tangible products, and there is therefore considerable freedom to tune the proposition – the content and commercial aspects of project design – to meet the needs of the client.

Contrast selling consultancy with the circumstances of someone selling chairs. They have only those chairs available from the factory to sell. Admittedly, they will probably be available in a variety of colours and styles, but if the customer wants something the factory doesn't make, then the salesperson is unlikely to make a sale.

The same is true, of course, for the consultant salesperson: if you cannot supply what the customer wants, then you will not make a sale. But selling consultancy involves the process of product specification. The consultant salesperson and the client work together to define the 'product' that the client is to buy. If this process is conducted well enough, then the consultancy will have created a proposition extremely attractive to the client. There is far more flexibility of design in consultancy than chairs, but to design an attractive proposition, you have to be able to identify what are the critical features for the client.

CRITICAL FEATURES OF A PROPOSITION

There are two aspects to a proposition:
1. *Its content*: this is the definition of the nature of the project, and the contribution the consultancy is going to make. This is usually embodied in *terms of reference*.
2. Its *commercial context*: this relates to fees, expenses, and other matters. This is usually embodied in *terms of business*.

In some major practices, different sales people deal with these two aspects separately.

There are thus many potential features of propositions that need to be clarified during the sales process. The question is, which of these is critical? Features that might be critical could be:
- a particular consultant undertakes the job personally;
- the sponsor's position is enhanced;
- the project commences on Monday;
- the consultant introduces a new technology to the factory;
- the price is less than £50,000.

Clients give you a lot of information when raising objections. For example, questions such as the following from the client will give you useful information about features they possibly consider important:
- 'Do you have sufficient international experience?'
- 'Will you be able to complete the project in three months' time?'
- 'Do you understand our industry/culture?'
- 'Aren't you expensive?'

You have, of course, to check whether these are serious questions, or simply incidental, during sales discussions.

Further information will emerge during negotiation. Negotiation takes place when two parties have decided, or are close to deciding, that they want to do business together. At its most basic it consists of bargaining or trading, but at its best it consists of the two parties working together to refine a proposition so that it has more benefits for both.

When selecting consultants, clients who opt for a more formal process of selection may well have a scoring system for assessing the relative merits of competitive proposals. It is useful to know what this is so that you can fashion an optimal proposition. Of course, there will be qualitative as well as quantitative criteria. Recently I heard of a major buyer of consultancy that had rejected the 'best' proposal in favour of the 'second best', as the client buying team believed they could work better with the latter.

Effective proposition design will not therefore automatically win sales, but it is a source of competitive advantage or disadvantage, and therefore has to be done well.

PITCHING FOR THE SALE

Your approach in pitching your proposition should be tailored to the buying process used by the client. You need to know how the buying decision is to be taken and the factors on which it is to be made. People who haven't met you will judge you only by your proposal; a presentation to an audience of decision makers or influencers can help in building their confidence and reducing their sense of uncertainty.

PREPARING A PROPOSAL

Whatever the selling or buying process being conducted, it is good practice to submit a written proposal, so that both you and the client have shared expectations of what is to be done.

The function of the proposal may vary from being simply written confirmation of what has already been orally agreed, to being the document on which the client is to make the buying decision. Some proposals may need to set out the rationale for carrying out the project in the first place (i.e. the need for it and the benefits of proceeding). This is required when, for example, the client or the client's colleagues need to be reassured of the value of the project. If this is not required, then you need only to describe how you will meet the needs defined by the client and the reasons why your consultancy practice is particularly well equipped to do so.

In taking the decision on what to include in your proposal, you need to consider the probable audience. What can they be safely assumed to know already? If in doubt, it is probably better to include explanatory material rather than leave it out.

Ideally, the proposal should serve to confirm that which has already been discussed, but it should also bring some added value to the client.

Some years ago some associates and I were commissioning a piece of consultancy, and our experience is instructive. We interviewed four firms. With one, the meeting was curtailed; the consultant made some disparaging remarks about a couple of our competitors. My associate asked for us to be excused for a moment. Outside the meeting he said, 'We can't possibly use him. What if he were to make similar remarks about us?' So we found an excuse to end the meeting.

A second consultant came from a large firm. Being ourselves a small firm, we had an uncomfortable (and possibly unfounded) feeling that we would not be treated with great importance because of our size.

We were left with two contenders, both of whom we invited to put in proposals. One firm, (Firm A), although we were not very taken with them at the outset, conducted a very good sales meeting; by the end, they were front runners. Then we received their proposals.

Firm A sent in a proposal that simply confirmed the project. It seemed very much like a boilerplate job – i.e. a standard proposal that had received some limited tailoring to meet our requirements. By contrast the other firm in the running – Firm B – produced a thoughtful proposal that really added value. It showed an appreciation of our circumstances, and contributed helpfully to our thinking, which gave us greater confidence in their ability to do the job. Had Firm A produced something half as good, they would have got the job; as it was, Firm B won the contract.

The message therefore is that you should seek opportunities to add value in a proposal. This can be by an insightful appraisal of a client's situation: helping the client to gain a clearer understanding of the circumstances in which you are going to deliver your consultancy services.

Sometimes it may be possible (and helpful) to prepare a proposal in draft and send this for comment to a close contact in the client organisation involved in the buying process. It can then be refined to meet the client's needs more closely. (This can be part of a sophisticated selling technique: by getting the client's involvement in producing the proposal, it is seen as a joint problem solving process rather than selling.)

PRESENTING THE PROPOSAL

A proposal is at least a written record of what has already been orally agreed with the client. A face to face presentation, however, allows the client to assess the individual consultants. It is a form of sales meeting, albeit structured in a format somewhat different from other meetings. The risk at this point is that you become 'proposal orientated': you regard the presentation as only an oral proposal. Remember that the presentation gives the client an experience of what it is like to work with you.

The practical aspects of presenting a proposition will be dealt with in the next chapter. Suffice it to say at this point that it is important to understand why the client is interested in a presentation, and what they hope to get out of it. You can then tailor your presentation against these criteria.

For example, we were presenting a proposal to a client and asked whether we could assume that the interview panel had read the proposal. We were assured they had and so we decided to run the meeting as a workshop, to help the client get a taste of how we worked. We won the sale.

ORGANISING FOR SELLING

Selling and operating will be done by the same person who is a sole practitioner but (perhaps) by different people in a large practice. It is in this latter case that problems of organising the sales function arise because of the variety of people who might be in contact with a client on just one single project.

This problem is compounded when:
- there are several projects in which the firm is engaged with a single client;
- there are several buyers of consultancy within the client organisation – e.g. different business divisions.

Should the firm attempt to co-ordinate all its engagements with the client through one of its own partners or directors? Alternatively, should it have different account managers to deal with the different parts of the business? Managers of consultancy practices have agonised over the type of organisation that is best. I know of one firm that tinkered with its structure twice a year in an attempt to optimise its performance – without success; it is now out of business.

There are some general principles that can suggest the structure and processes that should be followed.

ALL CONSULTANTS HAVE SOME RESPONSIBILITY FOR SELLING

Everybody in a consultancy practice should recognise the importance of selling, and should be encouraged to take some responsibility for it. Usually this is limited at the most junior levels to identifying sales opportunities with existing clients, with greater responsibilities for selling increasing with rank and experience.

NOT ALL CONSULTANTS HAVE THE DESIRE OR APTITUDE TO SELL

It necessarily follows that there has to be some distinction in roles and responsibilities. A practice may distinguish between:
- 'finders' (or 'hunters');
- 'minders' (or 'farmers');
- 'grinders' (the project team).

The targets and expectations of how consultants allocate their time might reflect this. Exhibit 6.5 below gives an example of this.

Exhibit 6.5 Budgets for finders, minders and grinders

		New sales	Extension sales	Fee-earning
Finder	Days allocated	120	40	40
	Days sold	600	400	40
	Conversion ratio	5	10	1
Minder	Days allocated	40	80	80
	Days sold	120	400	80
	Conversion ratio	3	5	1
Grinder	Days allocated	10	30	160
	Days sold	30	120	160
	Conversion ratio	3	4	1

In each case we assume that there are 200 days per annum to be allocated (the rest being given over to holiday, training, administration, product development, etc.). The 200 days are invested in different ways according to the role of the consultant. A key figure to monitor is the conversion ratio – the 'return on investment' for time. The figures shown in Exhibit 6.5 are illustrative only; each practice needs to work out what is realistic according to its experience, but it is worth noting that:
- finders are expected to be more skilled at selling than the others;
- time spent in extension selling (selling to existing clients) should yield better results than new sales;
- time allocated to fee earning is fully used as such. This means that for a grinder selling will be fitted around fee earning.

ALL CONSULTANTS ENGAGED ON PROJECTS SHOULD SEEK OUT AND IDENTIFY OPPORTUNITIES FOR FURTHER WORK FOR THE CONSULTANCY PRACTICE

Opportunities for further work with existing clients ('extensions') can arise from a variety of sources, most often concerning an aspect of a client's business that is causing dissatisfaction or an area for development. When such a possibility arises, the consultant should probe to find out what the real need is. Other points to consider are:
- Does the client consider the problem important?
- Does the client need external resources to resolve the problem?

A project team is well placed to identify extension opportunities; this topic should be on the agenda at each progress review meeting.

More generally, skill in identifying high quality extension opportunities should be an aspect against which the performance of all consultants is assessed. They can help in supporting extension selling by:
- providing intelligence;
- providing introductions to key members of client staff.

Once an opportunity has been identified, you need to decide in what way it should be best exploited. All extension business must go through the same qualification and conversion procedures as new business. Although a particular consultant may have identified the opportunity, there may be others within the practice who are better able to convert the opportunity into a profitable sale.

YOU HAVE TO BE CLEAR ON THE SALESPERSON'S CONTRIBUTION TO THE SELLING PROCESS

Only if you are clear on what you want the salesperson to contribute can you plan how to run the selling function.

If the salesperson is simply a broker between the resources of the consultancy and the needs of clients, what is their particular contribution? Is it knowledge of a business sector or a network of contacts? Is it insight into the applications of, say, business process re-engineering to organisations? Is it access to particular skills in the firm? Or a combination of some or all of these?

I have come across all these attributes in various amounts in consultancy salespeople in different practices. Each reorganisation emphasises a different aspect; this year we will be organised in market related teams, whereas last year we belonged to mini-practices based on different functional specialisations. The danger of frequent change is that in the new organisation the salesperson's assets (networks, leads, sales initiatives, etc.) built up over the previous period become devalued, and they have to start building afresh.

Another difficulty is that the salesperson may not see their role in the same way as the firm's management. It is all very well to claim that the salesperson should be the facilitator of the sale, but salespeople like to be heroes. They need their clear successes; facilitation does not provide this, so human nature will resist some types of organisational role.

Wittreich's rule number 3 (see Chapter 7) states that 'A professional service can only be purchased meaningfully from someone who is capable of rendering the service. Selling ability and personality by themselves are meaningless.' This means that it will always be difficult to organise a consultancy sales force along the lines of those for a tangible product.

Much of the work in sales management in a firm therefore consists of resolving the tensions between specialist and selling activities.

RESOURCING THE BID PROCESS

Bidding requires a finite time. For small projects, the salesperson and/or designated project manager may prepare the bid; in larger ones, there may need to be more people involved. Because of the pressure to keep up fee-earning time, it can be difficult to get consultants to work on a bid in some consulting practices.

But bidding is a project itself, and should be managed as such. The salesperson must make sure that they have the right resources to carry it out. This means in particular having consultants with the technical specialisms needed available to work on the bid. Ideally the bid team should form (the core of) the project team that is to undertake the assignment if it is won.

MONITORING SALES PERFORMANCE

Monitoring sales performance is important for two reasons:
- It shows what the level of future sales is likely to be, and where sales effort needs to be directed;
- Successful sales performance can be analysed to identify what were the reasons for success and hence provide a guide to good practice.

For the purposes of monitoring sales performance a client can be allocated to stages in the selling process as follows:
1. *Sales development:* When sales activities are aimed at developing a relationship with the client, but when there is no specific project in view.

2. *Prospect*: Where there is a specific project (or projects) in view, but for which the practice has not yet received a request for a proposal or invitation to tender from the client.
3. *Proposal:* A proposal has been submitted to the client that the practice should carry out a specific project.
4. *Sale:* When the client has accepted a proposal and it is now in the order book.

The whole process can be thought of as a leaky pipeline (see Exhibit 6.6); at each stage, potential clients will drop out until only a few are left that lead to sales. As well as clients arising from sales development, prospects and proposals may derive from direct enquiries. There will also be clients lost at each stage (called 'turn-downs') because, for example, the deferral or cancellation of a project, or a contract that is awarded to a competing provider of consultancy services. Exhibit 6.6 shows the ratios that were calculated in one consulting practice.

Exhibit 6.6 The sales pipeline

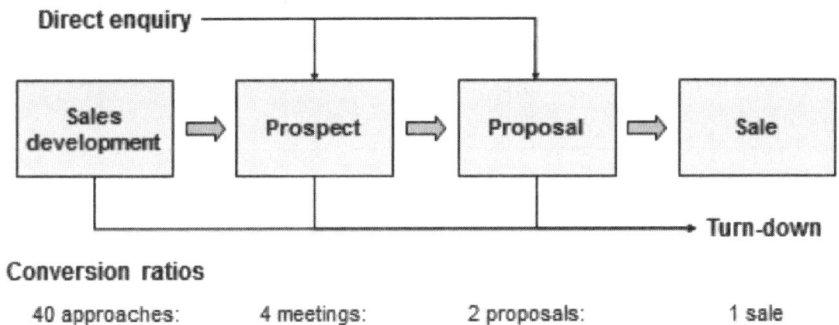

Clearly the ratios will vary with time, product, market and salespeople. On the figures shown, on an average of the 40 prospects only one resulted in a sale. The significance of this is that if you are to be a successful hunter:
- you have to start with a large number of organisations that you believe could be clients for your service;
- you have to accept a lot of 'noes' with only a few 'yeses'.

Sales performance will be measured by:
- the volume of business (number of clients, value of projects, etc.) at each stage in the sales process;
- the conversion of business from one stage to the next.

To this end, sales activity needs to be monitored, and examples of the type of information that can be recorded are shown in Figures 6.7–6.9. These show the information in tables which can be used as spreadsheets. (And of course there are proprietary sales management software programmes that perform the same task.) These should be updated regularly. The layout of the records means that the status of the sales process to a client can be quickly assessed, and action taken to follow up where required.

SALES DEVELOPMENT RECORD

Sales development is the development of a relationship with a potential client, targeted as being a likely buyer of your services. It should be the responsibility of a salesperson assigned to that target. A sales development record is shown on Exhibit 6.7.

Exhibit 6.7 Relationship development record

Account manager	Client	Current position	Next action	By when

It takes some time to develop clients in this category into prospects, and it is easy to let this category get too small. You should therefore review on a regular basis whether the level of activity in this category is sufficient.

PROSPECTS RECORD

Prospects can arise from either potential clients already identified in the sales development process or direct enquiries. New prospective projects with clients for whom you are currently working should be included here.

Exhibit 6.8 Prospects record

Account manager	Client	Possible project	Likely revenue	Probability	Current position	Next action	By when

The record in Exhibit 6.8 has spaces for the project for which the salesperson hopes the client will issue an invitation to tender, the likely revenue and an estimate of the probability that a sale will indeed follow. A separate calculation can then be made of the sum of the probable revenues, which gives a measure of the probable sales in the pipeline. This can be used as an indicator of possible future peaks and troughs of sales, which would have implications for revenue and resource utilisation. Again, you may prefer to use the EDIT process shown in Exhibit 6.4 to indicate the stage of maturity of any prospective opportunity.

PROPOSALS RECORD

Exhibit 6.9 Proposals record

Account manager	Client	Project	Value	Probability	Current position, competition etc	Next action	By when

The record in Exhibit 6.9 is similar to the prospects form, except that only firm proposals are recorded. Here, the sum of the probable sales is a good measure of future workload. Risks to monitor particularly on this record include:
- a high value proposal of low probability that will place a high demand on resources if it should sell;
- a low total probable revenue combined with high probabilities are a sign that future workload might be low if the probabilities have been over- estimated.

OTHER USES

It is important to monitor the conversion rate from one stage to the next. Key ratios to monitor are:
- Number of sales divided by number of proposals.
- Value of sales divided by value of proposals.

Typically in management consultancy these figures might be one-third to a half – i.e. only one in two or three proposals is accepted. If the ratio becomes too low, this can be a sign that either you are bidding for the wrong business, or that your proposals are insufficiently competitive. Likewise, a high conversion rate might indicate opportunities for business expansion.

Reasons for proposals being turned down should be monitored through win-lose reviews with the client so that conversion performance can be improved.

Of course, the records need to be kept up to date. This means being honest about those prospects that show no sign of turning into business. It is a matter of judgement which opportunities should remain on the Sales Development and Prospects records. You may wish to remove a prospective client from the sales records if the likelihood of any revenue deriving from the effort is low.

Finally, use these sales records as a basis for improvement. Review performance to find out what techniques are successful, and which clients are the best bets. Distinguish successful performance from unsuccessful, and so build up an understanding of what constitutes good selling practice for your consultancy firm.

DEVELOPING SALES PERFORMANCE

It is always fascinating to get feedback from clients on their perceptions of consultants. I belong to a group of freelance consultants who, from time to time, organise a clients' forum at which selected clients are invited to give feedback on their experience in using consultants. At one of these forums a client, who had invited tenders for a consultancy contract worth £500,000, commented on the mixture of responses he got. 'The worst compensated for their incompetence by their arrogance; they couldn't answer simple questions. The ones we appointed were the opposite – technically excellent. Moreover they were sensitive to the cost implications of the project and ensured we had the financial resources to implement the changes required.'

Another client commented, 'The consultant made it easy for us to buy – it was not hard work for us. At no time did we feel that we were being sold to.'

Consultancy firms nowadays often solicit feedback from prospects and clients on their performance, after a sales effort or on the completion of a project. Follow-up after a sales effort should be implemented irrespective of whether the effort resulted in success.

One head of a firm tells an interesting story concerning one of his fellow directors, who asked a prospect what had clinched the sale in favour of his own practice. The client replied, 'It's because your people looked more like a team than the competition.' The director probed to find out what had led the client to this conclusion. 'A very simple thing,' replied the client, 'When your competitors made their presentation two of their team gave a disparaging look concerning the third, who was presenting.'

How frightening to think that a major sale was affected by such a simple piece of body language! But what helpful intelligence in managing sales training.

One of my associates talks about organisations that seem to have a 'sales prevention department'. Presumably no organisation has the aim of preventing sales, any more than a salesperson would wish to have the negative effect quoted above.

Yet everybody who is involved in selling will have experienced occasions when they leave a sales meeting knowing that they have failed. The failure is not that the customer did not want to buy – that possibility has always to exist if you want to be anything more than a high pressure salesperson. The failure is because the customer might well have bought, but poor selling technique resulted in the salesperson failing to convert the opportunity to a sale.

There are no techniques that will guarantee success in selling consultancy every time. But a good management process, which enables lessons to be learned and applied from experience, will enhance selling performance. This is the subject of the next chapter.

7

CONDUCTING SPECIFIC SALES TRANSACTIONS

BECOMING A CONSULTANCY SALESPERSON

The revenue of a consultancy practice depends on sales but it is a rare business that receives enough orders without any selling effort, so one of the activities that consultants need to undertake is selling.

Career advance in any profession usually involves taking on commercial responsibilities, yet many professionals recoil when contemplating selling. Many will have originally dismissed it as a career and fewer still will have previous experience of selling.

By contrast, the addition of consultancy to the product portfolio of other businesses (such as IT companies) in recent years, however, has meant that established sales forces have needed to sell consultancy.

It is said that the skilled salesperson can sell anything, which implies that there is a set of selling skills that are universally applicable. Whether this is true is debatable. Certainly there will be salespeople who find little difficulty in making the transition to selling consultancy from selling more tangible items. But there are several significant differences between these activities, and understanding the implications of these differences will help in selling consultancy. Likewise, the consultant who has no previous selling experience needs some guidance as to the appropriate sales processes to use in selling consultancy. There are challenges for both.

CHALLENGES FOR THE EXPERIENCED SALESPERSON

Even products that can be customised are usually broadly predefined offerings, which may be tailored in detail to the specific needs of a client. Much of the time, consultancy is the opposite. It starts with identifying the needs of the client (or responding to a set of needs as embodied in an invitation to tender) and then putting together an offering that helps the client to address these needs.

This means that – unless you are a consultant with only one product – it is unusual to sell consultancy by going to a client with a fixed preconception of what you are going to sell them. Selling is more often about spotting opportunities than creating needs. The implications for you if you are a traditional salesperson are therefore:

- Each consultancy project is a uniquely tailored offering. A car salesman might sell from a product catalogue; the only variations are the extras that a customer might want. In consultancy, the sales process involves product definition.
- You must listen to clients' requirements and shape offerings that reflect their needs.
- If you work for a large firm of consultants, you cannot have a comprehensive knowledge across all fields of its consultancy offerings, and so you will need to involve specialists in support selling.

The role of salesperson in consultancy is more one of facilitator than 'hero'. You have to create opportunities that others will help to realise.

Exhibit 7.1 The selling spectrum

Product	**Material goods**	**Consultancy**
Nature of the product	Tangible	Intangible
Orientation	Transaction	Relationship
Who specifies it	Producer	Client
Sales preoccupation	What we want to sell	What the client wants to buy
Basis of evaluation	Quality of the product	Quality of the person

Exhibit 7.1 shows the critical dimensions in thinking about the role of the salesperson. The Exhibit shows two extremes; it is unlikely that any sales activity will be wholly at one end or the other, but will be somewhere in between. What the Exhibit points out, though, is the thrust in selling consultancy; for those whose experience lies in selling products, the challenge lies in moving towards the right in the diagram.

The spectrum of selling is shown from being transaction oriented to relationship oriented. A salesperson who is strongly transaction oriented will be impelled to close the sale. In an extreme form this is typical of the high pressure salesperson, who has a prime objective to ensure that you buy.

Salespeople who want repeat business recognise early in their careers that they cannot be wholly transaction oriented. Of course, the quotas and targets that they are set are usually related to sales volume – no points for having wonderful relationships and no sales – but they will be anxious to preserve a good relationship with their customers.

Consultancy, too, has quotas and targets, but the need for a good relationship is even greater than with other products. When buying a tangible item you can see an example of what you will get; in consultancy you buy only a promise. Even if the consultancy has a proven track record, this is no guarantee of success on this occasion; it simply reduces the sense of risk. So there has to be a high level of trust between the salesperson and their client. But as with other successful client relationships, once they are firmly established, consultancy clients become a fruitful source of continuing business.

CHALLENGES FOR THE TECHNICAL SPECIALIST

There are challenges for the technical specialist who takes on sales responsibilities. As for the salesperson, there will be some who make the transition very easily; others find it difficult to accept a sales role. Some specialists feel selling is 'unprofessional', and are most uncomfortable when called on to do it.

Exhibit 7.2 Factors influencing selling performance

In such circumstances they may rely on their technical expertise, or the warmth of their relationships with the client to secure the sale. But as Exhibit 7.2 shows, there are three factors that combine to influence the selling performance of a professional:

- *Technical skills*: The specialist skills of the consultant;
- *Interpersonal skills*: In the short term, these are the skills of conducting effective personal relationships. In the longer term, these are manifest as the consultant's network, which needs to be established, maintained and developed;
- *Selling skills*: Understanding buying and selling processes in consultancy, and capability in identifying opportunities and developing sales.

All three are important. The area of the triangle in Exhibit 7.2 depends on the length of all three sides, so if the length of one side is nil, then the area will be nil. If the area of the triangle represents sales performance, all three skills must be represented to achieve a satisfactory standard of sales performance. What consultants and other professionals often feel reluctant to admit is that selling skills are important. The Exhibit shows, however, that selling skills are as important as the other two.

THE INGREDIENTS OF SELLING PERFORMANCE

Let's now consider each of the factors shown in Exhibit 7.2.

TECHNICAL SKILLS CREATE REPUTATION

Ultimately, the capacity to execute projects well will be the determinant of a consultancy practice's success. Reputation counts for a lot; in my first week as a consultant I was told, 'One bad job costs 100 good ones'. Satisfied clients act as connectors to fresh business; and satisfied executives who change jobs introduce their favoured consultants to their new employers. Technical skill creates a favourable reputation, which helps the extrinsic selling process mentioned in Chapter 6.

INTERPERSONAL SKILLS CREATE A NETWORK

Most consultancy sales arise from existing customers so experienced sales people recognise the need for their activities to be relationship rather than transaction-led if they are to achieve more than a single sale. Research supports common sense that we will buy more from the salesperson we like than from one to whom we are indifferent, other factors being equal.

But because of the nature of the consultancy product, far more emphasis has to be placed on the relationship. The reason is that despite references and reputation, when a client buys a consultancy assignment, it is on trust. The project may be expensive and of considerable moment; a buyer may have staked their reputation on its success. Before doing this, they must have the confidence that it will be successful. It is unlikely that this will be the case unless there is a good relationship with the consultant. This relationship has to be underwritten by good work, however. If the consultant (or consultancy) has previously carried out high quality work, the client will be more inclined to give them more, hence the evidence that the greater part of consultancy work derives from existing or previous clients.

During your work, you will build up a network of relationships with people who are employed by past or prospective clients, professional contacts and so on. 'Networking' is about maintaining these relationships.

This can be done quite easily, by attending business or professional meetings, or even informally over lunch. I remember sitting at lunch with a partner in a firm of consultants (with whom I was networking!) who complained about his consultant team: 'As we sit here, they are all sat at their desks eating sandwiches. Why aren't they out networking?'

Some 80-90 per cent of a consultancy's sales come from its network – some two-thirds of this from repeat business and the remainder from referrals. Even if the activity is not directly related to a sale, there are benefits in networking:

- Getting market intelligence;
- Obtaining leads and introductions;
- Raising awareness of your firm and its services;
- Maintaining the network.

So consultants have to be active in creating and maintaining their networks. Even so, time spent on networking has to be invested with a purpose; it is easy to be a busy fool, and there are people who are time-wasters, as there are in any other area of activity; beware of them.

SELLING SKILLS ARE NEEDED TO CREATE SALES

Shortly after I started my first job as a management consultant there was one of those periodic downturns in the market. All consultants are exhorted to sell, and in a recession we were doubly so. Being young and enthusiastic, I started to try to sell to my (limited) network. My sales patter was simple: 'Consultancy is jolly good, and so is my firm. Why don't you buy a project?'

I was totally unsuccessful, because I had no selling skills. The unhappy truth is that technical skills and a good relationship will create few sales by themselves. Selling skills are also required and the remainder of this chapter deals with this topic.

PURPOSES OF SELLING – WHAT WE ARE TRYING TO ACHIEVE

The simple explanation of 'what we are trying to achieve' is a sale. But as we have seen in Chapter 6, it is rarely a single stage process – there are several steps and these form the basis of a conversion process.

Conversion is the activity of developing opportunities to successive stages of the sales process. The skills of doing this are in conducting key transactions with the prospective client; these are covered later in this chapter. Suffice to repeat that it is sensible to monitor your success at conversion at each stage of the sales process, and to research the reasons for success or failure. By monitoring conversion performance you can identify areas of strength and weakness, and develop a better idea of what practices will help you to optimise your conversion rate.

But conversion is not adequate by itself. You need also to qualify: qualification involves choosing which prospective clients to pursue. This is important because it relates to the effective use of time. The consultancy sales person should be devoting their time to pursuing those prospects that are most likely to produce sales.

QUALIFICATION

At each stage of the sales process there is a need for qualification: deciding where to invest your time and effort. You need to decide which opportunities should be converted to the next stage of the sales process, or which sales opportunities with a particular client should be pursued.

Obviously, clients may disqualify themselves: a sales call may be unsuccessful, or a prospect may not agree to a meeting. What is particularly hard for the salesperson, however, is to disqualify an opportunity from the consultancy's point of view. It is hard because the salesperson may well have put much effort in to nursing the prospect to this stage in the sales process.

There are several obvious reasons for disqualification. Some people love to chat to consultants and to pick their brains, with no real intention of offering an assignment. Likewise, if the project in view is one that the consultancy cannot do, or is of questionable ethics, or involves an actual conflict of interest, then the opportunity may also be disqualified.

Early in the sales process, therefore, you should assess the probability of a consultancy project deriving from your efforts. To this end, you should check that:
- there is a genuine need for consultancy work of the kind that the consultancy can offer;
- the prospective client intends to offer this to outside consultants;
- the individuals with whom you are dealing have the budget and authority to proceed with the project, or can act as connectors to such individuals.

Qualification is even more crucial at the time of preparing a proposal, not only because the task is time consuming, but also because the proposal is a commitment by the consultancy to carry out a specified project.

Before offering to submit a proposal, therefore, you should consider:

- Is the consultancy able to carry out the work, in terms of the competence and availability of resources?
- What are the risks involved, and are they acceptable? Risks to be considered include:
  - the financial standing of the client and hence their ability to pay the fees required;
  - political risks;
  - the difficulty of achieving the project deliverables;
  - the complexity and size of the project.
- Will undertaking the project produce any *actual* conflicts of interest in respect of any existing clients?
- Will undertaking the project produce any conflicts of interest with other parts of the consultancy?
- Is there a serious chance of winning the assignment?

Salespeople are strongly impelled to make sales and so there is the temptation to bid in response to every invitation to tender. The failure to qualify properly, however, can result in either wasting time, or committing to projects that are unprofitable at best.

DEMONSTRATING THE QUALITY OF YOUR CONSULTANCY IN THE SALES PROCESS

Consultancy may appear to a client to be an undifferentiated product; if the client has specified what is to be achieved and the steps towards this, any capable consultant could probably deliver. Differentiation must therefore lie not only in the consultancy service, but also in the quality of its delivery.

Differentiation of delivery starts in the sales process, so what should you be seeking to achieve in this?

Beginners in selling often believe that a client will be persuaded to buy through references from other clients, product knowledge, and technical skills. Collectively, in the sales jargon, these can be called 'proofs', and they are undoubtedly important. They must, however, be complemented by skill in conducting the sales process; both are vital.

Wittreich, in a seminal article in Harvard Business Review in 1966 (*How to Buy/Sell Professional Services*, Harvard Business Review, March 1966), suggested there were three objectives in selling professional services to be kept in mind:

1. *'Minimizing uncertainty:* A professional service must make a direct contribution to the *reduction of the uncertainties* involved in managing a business. The proper assessment of a service, unlike tangible goods,

usually must take into account the impact of its performance on the client's business.
2. *Understanding problems:* A professional service must come directly to grips with a fundamental problem of the business purchasing that service. The successful performance of the service, far more so than the successful production of a product, depends on an understanding of the client's business.
3. *Buying the professional:* A professional service can only be purchased meaningfully from someone *who is capable of rendering the service.* Selling ability and personality by themselves are meaningless.'

The importance of these concepts has been regularly endorsed by research in the UK. In the early editions of this book, a study by KPMG in 1988 was quoted; in 2005 further research was carried out by the then Institute of Management Consultancy, which showed much the same results. (And there is little evidence to show that these factors have since changed!) It showed that the relative importance of factors involved in selecting a management consultancy was as shown in Exhibit 7.3.

Exhibit 7.3 Important factors in selecting a management consultancy

- People
- Sector experience
- Functional experience
- Existing relationship
- Price
- Brand
- Other

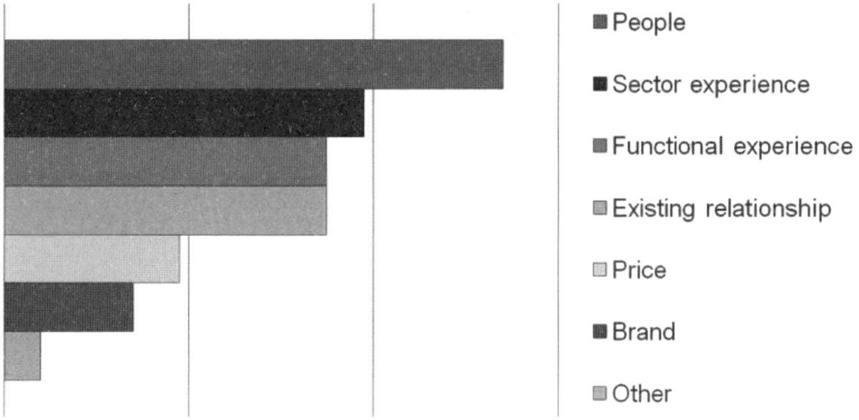

Based on research by Penna for the Institute of Management Consultancy:

As ever, the quality of the people is a strong deciding factor – Wittreich's third objective. In a large consultancy practice, however, the person who is the account manager (maybe a partner or director of the practice) will not necessarily be delivering the service. This is when team selling is used, which is covered later in this chapter.

Although fee levels are shown in Exhibit 7.3 to be less important comparatively, they can be instrumental in the buying decision in competition when:
- other features of competing firms are very similar;
- there is a significant difference in the amounts quoted.

The fact that 'previous work with client' comes so low seems to contradict the comments made elsewhere about existing clients being the most fertile ground. The same survey, however, notes that 'Business colleagues were the most important source of information about management consultancies'. Previous work together may not be significant in the intrinsic selling process (i.e. to win a particular assignment), but is important in getting you through the door in the first place (i.e. being invited to tender) – the extrinsic selling process.

THE SALES PROCESS

KEY STEPS IN THE SELLING PROCESS

Of course there are direct enquiries from clients, when they call you up or send an invitation to tender. In this section, however, we assume that the sales have to be generated by the sales activity of the consulting practice alone.

There are three key steps involved in practical selling:
1. Identifying potential clients, getting access to them and establishing a dialogue with them.
2. Conducting sales transactions (telephone calls, correspondence, meetings), which should lead to an invitation to tender (ITT). An ITT need not be a formal document – it can be an oral request from a prospect for you to put in a proposal.
3. Converting the ITT to a sale.

The framework within which these activities are applied may be ad hoc, or it may be part of a focused, proactive sales campaign to get new clients.

Large consultancies with extensive networks may have no difficulty getting access to a specific target. With greater resources than small practices, they may invest more in selling to a specific target prospect. For example, they may prepare a detailed presentation, free of charge, on an aspect of the client's business where the consultancy believes there to be a good opportunity of working together. Even with good contacts, however, the number of times you can 'cash in' on a relationship is limited. You can schedule meetings with a key contact about a couple of times a year, but goodwill on their side will disappear if they see the meetings are of little value.

Selling skills are needed in all cases. In what follows I have assumed that you cannot command the attention of the target and so have to follow a more general sales process.

MANAGING THE SELLING PROCESS

Early in the selling process you will need to judge how much work (for example, how many meetings) is required to win an invitation to tender. In some circumstances the opportunity may arise at the first meeting; this will be the case when your consultancy offering is clearly defined and you have carefully pre-qualified the prospect. For example, a recruitment consultant may have established the prospect's need for recruitment services during a preliminary telephone call. At the initial meeting the consultant will have sold the firm's services extrinsically, so that the prospect feels encouraged to invite the consultant to submit a proposal if there is a vacancy to be filled.

In other cases a series of meetings may be required, to do one or more of the following:
- Clarify the nature of the consulting project;
- Meet others of the client staff who might be involved in the buying process;
- Introduce others from the consultancy to help with selling or who might be involved in operating the project.

Remember the criteria that:
- the client has to recognise that a problem or opportunity exists;
- the client has to believe that it merits attention;
- the client must believe that it is possible to resolve the problem or realise the opportunity;
- the client must see the value of outside consultancy help;
- the client must choose your help.

Remember that it is a competitive market. As well as managing your side of the sales process, you need to be convincing the prospect that you are the right consultancy to undertake the project.

ESTABLISHING A DIALOGUE WITH A PROSPECTIVE CLIENT

In establishing a dialogue with a prospective client, there are three steps:
1. Identify the prospect organisation to which you wish to sell.
2. Find out which person you should contact.

3. Approach the prospect with the aim of winning a meeting at which you can present your services.

IDENTIFYING PROSPECTS

If clients are not forming a queue at your door to do business with you (and if they are, why not put up your fees?) then you have to find new clients. Let us assume that you have to find these by hunting. You need to know what you are looking for, so you should draw up a prospect profile, i.e. the key characteristics of an organisation likely to buy your services.

You then have to identify the organisations and individuals within them where you have a good chance of being able to sell your services. One useful way of doing this is to do mystery shopping; imagine you are a potential customer or investor in this sort of business and then do a web search for businesses that meet these criteria. Trade associations are also a good way of finding organisations that meet your target profile. And of course there are a host of online databases that you can search that will also help.

However, there are two other requirements: the organisation must have a need for your services, and you have to find someone you can contact whom you can use as a link to the organisation.

The need for your services depends on what they are, of course. Are they services that all organisations might need (e.g. recruitment consultancy – although that might be segmented by job type or industry) or are they ones that are used to support a specific project or development initiative? And even if there is a need for your services, are these services already being supplied by a competitor? (It can be difficult to displace an incumbent supplier. Indeed, you need to take care that the client is not simply conducting some market testing as a means of checking their preferred supplier!)

You can find these out most easily by entering a dialogue with someone who is in an appropriate role in the target prospect.

So the next stage is to approach the prospect.

WHO TO SELL TO

Whereas organisations may have sophisticated systems for specifying and purchasing hardware, these are rarely matched by the processes for buying consultancy. In selling consultancy, you may find yourself in the position of having to guide the prospect through the buying process. The consultancy sales process is directed towards this, involving, as it does, clarifying exactly what the prospect wants.

(It is worth noting, however, that as consultancy has become a major item of expense for organisations, the purchasing process has come under greater scrutiny. There is a trend towards 'rules based purchasing', led by the public sector, which is intended to provide better value for money and fairer treatment of suppliers. Purchasing departments have yet, however, to develop appropriate methods for buying consultancy in a way that allow for the fact that it is not a commodity, finding it difficult to discriminate on anything other than price.)

The old adage in selling is 'sell to the MAN, the person who has the Money, Authority and Need.' In an organisation of any size, these may be different individuals or a variety of committees. Miller and Heiman have identified the following key prospect roles in the buying process:
- The *user*(s) of the service;
- The *technical buyer*, whose approval is needed, acting as a gatekeeper;
- The *economic buyer*, whose authority is needed to release the funds.

It is difficult if not impossible to identify these from outside, and so the fourth role of *coach* is important. The coach is the member of the prospect organisation who is committed to your consultancy's offering and who can provide guidance to (and perhaps influence over) those filling the other key roles.

If you have immediate access to a powerful chief executive as your buyer then this distinction of role is less relevant. In other cases you need to recognise the roles, and the buying process that will be engaged. For example, the situation where a client has been commissioned by her board to carry out a study of IT requirements for her business needs a quite different selling process from trying to sell a study on IT to a client who is satisfied with her present arrangements.

An important objective early in the sales process is therefore to obtain intelligence about the buying process and the roles of the interested parties. This will enable you to focus your selling effort to best effect.

APPROACHING THE PROSPECT

It is an unusual prospect who would engage management consultants without first meeting them – and an unusual firm of consultants who would agree to work with a client under these conditions. So meetings are an essential part of the selling process. The purpose of the approach is therefore to secure a selling meeting, preferably with the MAN, who of course could be a woman. You may need to do some preliminary research on who might be the MAN, and receptionists and other support staff can be helpful in guiding you to the right person. In situations of any complexity, it may be necessary to identify a coach (see above) as a first step.

Of course, it is far easier to approach a prospect through an introduction rather than by cold calling. Networking web sites such as LinkedIn enable you to identify individuals who work for the prospect and also those among your direct contacts who might effect an introduction.

CONDUCTING SELLING TRANSACTIONS

PLANNING A CONTACT DISCUSSION – SETTING TARGETS

You are unlikely to make a significant sale to a new client in the course of a single contact. You will advance to a degree (you hope) at each contact; and by a series of advances achieve a sale. Advance is through a series of discussions – whether by mail, phone or meeting.

In planning each contact discussion you need to have an idea of where you are starting from, and to set a realistic target of how far you might get in this discussion. It is also sensible to think about:
- Stretch targets: how far can you go if things are going well?
- Fall-back targets: what is the minimum you expect to achieve from the discussion?

Exhibit 7.4 Setting targets for a discussion

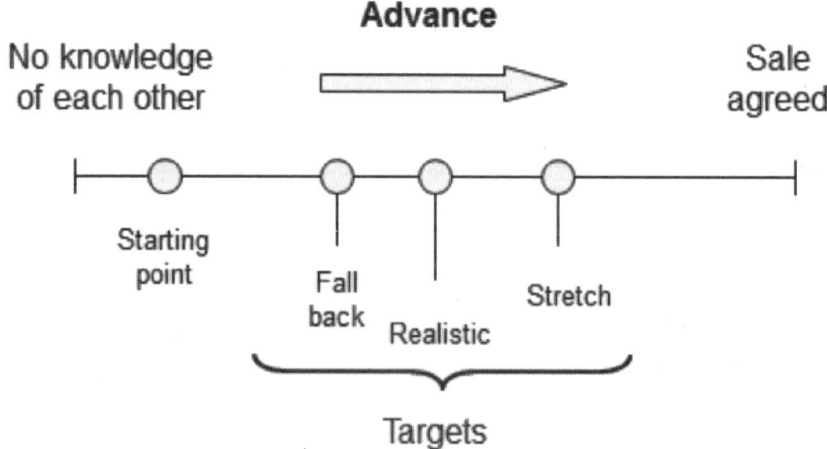

Exhibit 7.4 illustrates the process. At the left hand side is shown the situation where client and consultancy have no knowledge of each other; at the right hand side is where they have agreed on a sale.

The advantage of setting stretch and fall-back targets is that they encourage a more positive frame of mind. With a single target you either make it, or you don't. Under these circumstances it is tempting to set the target low and hence have a better chance of beating it. By contrast, a range of targets enables you to cope with the unexpected during a discussion, without a sense of 'failure'.

There are two main areas in which you need to consider targets:
1. *Conversion and qualification*: The buying process is the mirror of the sales process. Both aim to establish whether the client and consultancy firm should work together. The conversion and qualification process proceed hand in hand: when the buyer qualifies the consultant to the next stage of the buying process, then the consultant has converted the client to the next stage of the sales process, and vice versa.
2. *Information gathering*: You need data to:
   - specify the nature of the work to be undertaken;
   - inform the conversion and qualification processes;
   - understand the context of the sale – for example, the key players, the political environment, the current business challenges and priorities.

The detailed nature of the targets will change as the sale progresses, and they will have a significant influence over what is discussed: the agenda for the contact discussion. But the pursuit of an agenda willy-nilly will have a poor effect on the client relationships.

Although most important at the start of the sales process, relationships remain important throughout. Every contact has an impact on the relationship, and so you need to consider how to ensure that relationships continue to develop favourably throughout and avoid selling activities that may have a negative effect on them, for example, by pressurising the client to buy.

HOW TO APPROACH A PROSPECT

Having identified a prospective client, you have to decide how you will approach them. Should you telephone and ask for an appointment, or do you need to warm them up with a letter or email beforehand?

Exhibit 7.5 illustrates a simple model for developing business with a new client:

Exhibit 7.5 Developing business with a new client

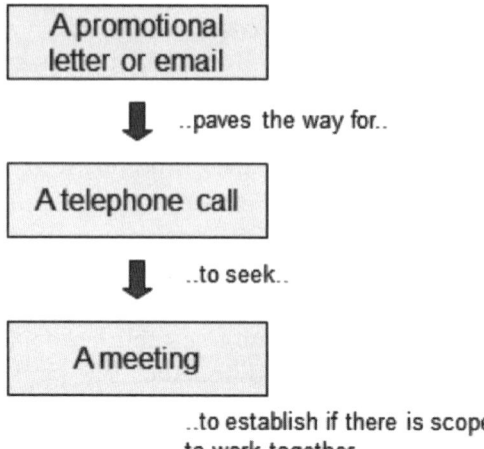

Part of the promotional activity of larger consultancies is to circulate their own publicity literature, such as newsletters or business journals to prospective clients. This means that there will already be some awareness among prospects about the firm and its services. If this is the case, then there may be no need to warm up with a preliminary contact.

Even so, promotional material might provide a convenient reason for contacting a client in the first place. For example, you may have recently published a newsletter highlighting a particular project you have carried out. Your email or letter might suggest (with good reasons!) why such a project might be of interest to the recipient. (Incidentally, there is a school of thought that sending a letter rather than an email might result in more attention. Nowadays, there is so much junk email that unless the recipient knows you there is a good chance that no attention will be paid to an email message).

Publicity material may have some sort of call to action that invites a response and a mechanism for so doing (e.g. a phone number to call, a link to a web site or an email address to find out more). This means that if approaches are focused on those who have shown interest, a better conversion ratio should result.

The objective in warming up the prospect is to provide enough information to convince them of the benefits of investing time in a telephone conversation, and become inclined towards the idea of meeting you. You are seeking, in fact, to satisfy the qualification process on the prospect's side. If your service can be explained and understood in a simple telephone conversation, this might be the best method of qualification. If it is complicated, or you feel uncomfortable at a direct approach, then written communication might be best. You must also consider what you are offering at the first meeting – what are the benefits to the prospect in meeting you? Some executives may be prepared to make time to see consultants speculatively, but rarely simply to hear them give a catalogue of their services. They need to know how the consultancy's services are going to develop business performance and competitiveness, or remedy problems. Sometimes consultants may offer an appraisal of (some aspect of) the business early in the relationship as an incentive. For example, a strategy consultancy might make a presentation on a business's position within its sector, hoping to display a knowledge and capability that will persuade the prospect to do business with them.

If the presentation is to be effective, then the consultancy has to invest time in preparing it. Time should not be invested lightly; the selling team should feel that it is worthwhile. The presentation is therefore unlikely to be made at the first meeting between consultancy and prospect.

THE TELEPHONE CALL

Although telephone technique is a basic selling skill, it is one in which I have found experienced consultants often to be weak. The following notes are therefore intended to summarise the key points.

One of the first challenges is getting through to speak to potential customers at a prospect. If they are warmed up and expecting you to call, then there is less difficulty. Even so it can be difficult to find a time when the executive is free to speak to you. As a salesperson you will want to keep the initiative and therefore will want to make the call yourself. If there is little incentive for a prospect to call back, it is unlikely they will do so. You have to make the call at times when you are free, so you need to know when the executive is likely to be free to receive it. It is best to avoid the core times for meetings: 10am-12pm and 2pm- 4pm. Some consultants try to phone before 9am or after 6pm because they might get through straight away at those times. Even so, my rule of thumb is that it often takes several telephone calls before you can get to speak to a prospect, even if you are calling their mobile phone.

A further hint is to telephone after the hour or half hour rather than before (i.e. at 10.35 rather than 10.25). Meetings usually start on the hour or half hour, so even if you get through at 10.25am, the prospect may be about to go off to a meeting, and so have little time to speak. This is less likely to be the case at 10.35am.

Personal assistants and secretaries (although an increasingly rare breed) are more often helpful than obstructive; ideally, you should make them your ally in the selling process. Occasionally one might be too protective, asking your business and judging that it is unlikely to be of interest to the boss. If it really is impossible to get past the PA, or enlist their help, you can:

- Abandon this prospect – invest your time in others that might offer a better chance of a sale. After all, an executive's PA should be able to tell the difference between interesting and unwanted approaches.
- Try to bypass the PA. You need to be convinced of the error of their judgement. Moreover, it could be embarrassing to end up talking to them again despite trying to bypass them.
- Find a different point of access. This could be via another executive in the same organisation, seeking an introduction through a mutual acquaintance, or aiming to 'bump into' the executive or an appropriate connector at some business or social function.

A PA can be helpful in easing communication if the executive is proving inaccessible. A comment from the consultant might be: 'I wrote to Jean Brown last week concerning our services, which we thought might be of particular value to your business at this time. In my letter I said I'd phone to see whether we might meet and to fix a mutually convenient time'.

In my experience, the PA response might be:
- 'Yes, she's asked me to fix a meeting when you rang' (great!);
- 'She asked me to tell you that she's not interested';
- 'She's not spoken to me about it'.

In the last case you might then ask the PA to find out what the boss wants to do, so that if she is not available next time you ring, at least you can stop wasting time if they are not interested. But this is very much a fall-back position if you can't get hold of the boss in the first place. Nowadays, of course there is a good chance that you don't actually talk to a human being, but engage with voice mail. Again, you should maintain the initiative – leave a message explaining why you are calling and say when you might call again. If you fail to make contact again, then suggest that the client calls you if they are interested. If they don't call, it means they are not interested and you can avoid wasting more time.

PREPARING FOR THE TELEPHONE CALL

Before placing the call, you have to have prepared what the structure of the telephone conversation is going to be. Preparing what you are going to say is only half the telephone conversation. What are you aiming to find out, as well as to convey, in this conversation? You will want to confirm your understanding of the prospect's needs, the position of your contact in the buying process, and the next steps, at the very least. This is to enable you to qualify the prospect for the next stage.

You will also want to set some objectives for the discussion. There is a series of possible outcomes from a telephone approach:
1. Receive an invitation to tender.
2. Fix a meeting with the prospect.
3. A meeting is to be arranged at some future date.
4. Send material then contact again.
5. Call back at a specified time in future.
6. No interest.

It is unlikely that you get an invitation to tender because the prospect has an immediate need for your services. Even if you did, you would want to qualify this – you are unlikely to put in a proposal without first meeting the prospect.

Next best is that the prospect agrees to a meeting; you have achieved your objective in the telephone approach. The remaining outcomes are of decreasing commercial attractiveness. The reason for showing them, however, is that the outcome is not limited to a simple 'yes/no' to a meeting. Even if there is no interest in your services now, you may have created a link that brings a prospective client into your network – a link you could probably nurture and exercise profitably at some time in the future.

CONDUCTING SALES MEETINGS

Having got access to your target prospect, the next step is to try to persuade the prospect to invite you to tender for a piece of consultancy work. This is accomplished by conducting one or a series of sales meetings.

Of these meetings, the most important is the initial contact made with each person involved in the buying process: '*You never get a second chance to make a first impression.*' Better selling performance derives from stacking the odds more in your favour. The better the first impression, the better the chance of winning the sale. The first meeting, therefore, will have a profound effect on what follows, which is why this is the one on which we will concentrate. Obviously all the others will have some impact, but they will only modify that created at the first. Moreover, the first meeting will be significant as it will be largely instrumental in defining the general areas in which client and consultancy are to work together.

The relationship dimension is crucial; for example, the salesperson who catechises a senior executive to identify the focus of a project may damage the relationship. Any meeting with a client will affect the relationship with the consultant, and so meetings must have a relationship objective as well as that of content. It may be more worthwhile to establish a good long-term relationship than win an immediate sale.

Preparation for a sales meeting

Most consultants will nod vigorously when asked, 'Should you prepare for a sales meeting?' but will disagree on what form that preparation should take.

If Wittreich's third criterion is to be satisfied (see above), the consultancy salesperson has to be more than simply a broker of useful resources; you have to show the value of the connection between the needs of the prospect's business and the services of the consultancy – for example how your services will help the prospect address current key business issues. Nevertheless, as in the telephone conversation, you must avoid a preoccupation with what you are going to say. There is more extensive comment on the agenda for the first meeting below; for now, you should consider what you need to find out from the prospect, as well as what to say. The quality of questions and comments can serve to impress the prospect (and poor quality quite the opposite!)

Consequently you need to consider whether you need to take something along to the first meeting. One of my associates recommends that at the very least you take a printed sheet with a list of points for discussion – not necessarily as formal as an agenda – to the first meeting. The aim is to show that you have given some thought to this particular meeting; it is not merely a repeat of a score of similar meetings you have conducted over the previous months.

Personal impact

The salesperson in consultancy is initially the embodiment of the product. In selling a tangible item, it can be described and displayed. Not so in consultancy: the prospect will endow the consultancy service with the characteristics of the salesperson. Inevitably, the initial meeting will provide the client with a sample experience of working with you.

Consultants learn early in their careers how to dress properly, how to relate to clients and how to manage their body language. These requirements are as relevant to selling as they are to delivering consultancy projects. It is important to recognise that people take in information through what they see, hear and feel, and use all three channels. People have preferences, so each salesperson will have their own preference. The danger is that you will then use that channel exclusively; this will be all right with clients who have the same preference, but less effective with those whose preference is different. So you need to consider visual aids, the words you use, and the rapport you generate with the prospect.

Opening the sales meeting

For those new to selling, there is a problem about what to say after the initial pleasantries. Exhibit 7.6 suggests an outline agenda for an initial meeting.

Exhibit 7.6 Outline agenda for an initial meeting

1. **Pleasantries.**
2. **Bridge to the business discussion.**
3. **Probing for prospects' concerns.**
4. **Discussing how these concerns might be jointly addressed.**
5. **Decide next steps.**

As with meeting anybody for the first time, a meeting will open with pleasantries, to start building a personal relationship. Get the prospect talking early on; just because you have an agenda doesn't mean you have to do all the talking!

There then needs to be a natural bridge to talking about business. This needs to be done by body language as well as orally. Opening a notebook, for example, will serve to show that the business of the meeting is going to start.

Some years ago, I had reached this point in my first meeting with a finance director of a prospective client, to whom I had been introduced by the personnel manager, who reported to him. I had some previous discussions with the personnel manager who, I assumed, had briefed the FD. We then commenced the meeting and I proceeded on from the discussions I had with the personnel manager. After about 15 minutes, the FD stopped and said, 'Hang on a minute; what are we talking about here? I'm lost'. The personnel manager had not briefed him, and that was the last meeting I had with that prospect.

With that experience behind me, I favour a recap on the background to the meeting as an introduction to the business discussion. This serves to make sure that both you and the prospect are starting from the same point – a rendezvous, if you like. If it is a first meeting, it is also helpful for you and your prospect each to give a brief summary of your business and where you fit into it.

A technique that salespeople are sometimes taught is to take 'control' of a meeting. What this means in practice is controlling the agenda. Personally as a prospective client, I'm not sure I would want to be controlled. The prospect will be coming to the sales meeting with an agenda, even if it is not articulated. The good salesperson will allow for the fact that the prospect has an agenda and will let them express it. So early in the meeting you will perhaps wish to agree with the client on the points you are going to cover. It is also worthwhile checking how long the meeting is expected to last. The consultant is likely to have more experience in engaging in these meetings than the client, so needs to be an expert navigator!

These first items on the agenda are relatively uncontentious and will serve to help build rapport. Next you have to start to probe for the prospect's concerns and show how your services relate to them. (The probing pyramid technique, set out below, can be used for structuring this part of the meeting.) Finally, as shown in Exhibit 7.6, you have to agree on the next steps to be taken by both sides following the meeting, which ideally should take the selling process on to the next stage.

The probing pyramid: how to establish the prospect's needs

It can be difficult, however, to decide what questions to ask. What do you need to know? What kind of questioning should you use?

The 'probing pyramid' helps to identify the prospect's needs. Although a simple model, it can provide the basis for an extensive discussion. Once the probing pyramid is understood and put into action, it provides you with both the types of question to ask and the order in which they might be asked, as the meeting – or series of meetings – progresses. It is particularly useful in planning the first meeting with a new prospect.

Exhibit 7.7 The probing pyramid

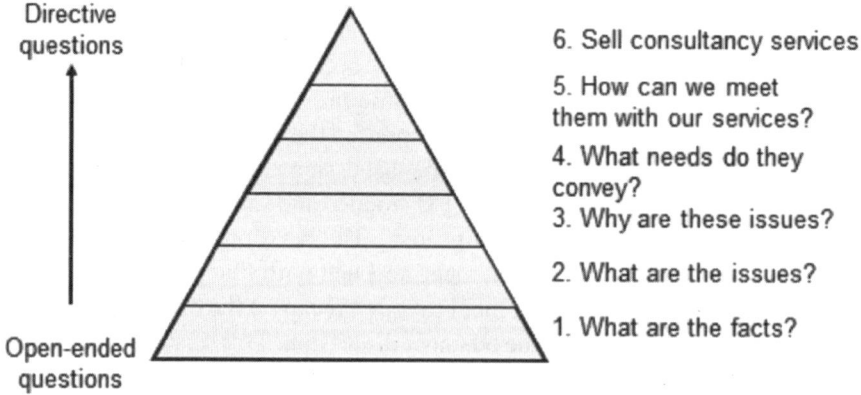

The framework is shown in Exhibit 7.7. The sequence of the agenda is shown on the right. At the start you may discuss facts about the business, but then you need to move on to the issues affecting the business.

There are two potential traps at this stage, in that it is tempting:
- having identified one issue, then to proceed with the next stages. At an initial meeting, if you are to identify other relevant issues, note each issue, and then remain at item 2 in the agenda until you have exhausted this topic, or make sure that you return to it.
- To leap straight from item 2 to item 5 without going through items 3 and 4. Items 3 and 4 enable you to shape your response in item 5 in a way that will be attractive to the prospect.

CONVERTING THE ITT TO A SALE

An invitation to tender (ITT) can arise early or late in a sales process and have tight or loose specifications. Exhibit 7.8 illustrates progressive tightness of specifications.

Exhibit 7.8 Progressive precision of specification

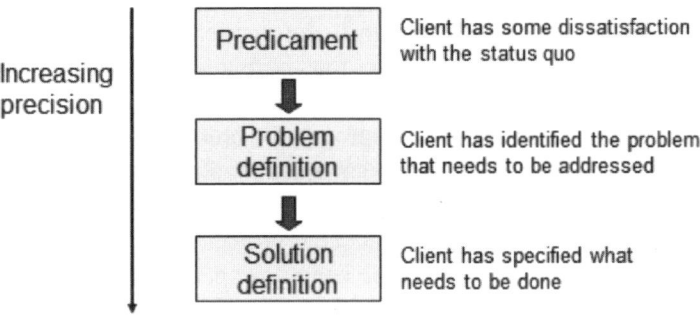

An example of the invitations to tender at each stage for a consultancy practice could be:

Predicament: How can we sell more to our clients?
Problem definition: How can we develop the performance of our account managers?
Solution definition: Can you deliver a training course for account managers?

A client might be at any of these stages when opening a discussion with a consultant; and the degree of definition may progress during the sales process. Indeed, there is some truth in the saying that 'selling is free consultancy', but beware of providing excessive value free of charge in order to win a sale. For example, coming up with a robust definition of what the underlying problem is following the client's predicament definition may involve both considerable research and effort.

An explanation of how to conduct this process is given in Chapter 2 on problem solving; suffice to say that there comes a point when you and the client have agreed that you should submit a proposal.

In the sales process (see Chapter 6) this is divided into two parts:

- **proposition design,** which is about the content of your response;
- **pitching**, which is how you put it across to the client.

The former is dealt with in more detail in Chapter 3 on terms of reference; the latter is dealt with in more detail below. But first, a word of warning:

consultants invest a lot of time and effort in preparing proposals, but often the client will have already a predilection to buy - or not - depending on the consultant's performance in the earlier stages of the sales process. So make sure that you put in sufficient effort early in the sales process.

SUBMITTING A PROPOSAL

The proposal is often the only significant written communication in the sales process. Terms of reference set the content and terms of business set the commercial context for a consultancy project. These are usually brought together in a single document – the proposal – prepared by the consultancy.

As well as being a contractual document, a proposal has a selling purpose. It must:
- persuade the client to undertake the project (or to endorse a decision already made), setting out the benefits expected;
- make the case for engaging consultants;
- set out how the consultancy would approach the assignment;
- convince the client that the consultancy is well equipped to carry out the assignment, and that it should be chosen to do so;
- lay out the terms on which the assignment is to be conducted.

The length, form and complexity of proposal documents will vary widely according to what is appropriate but, in varying degrees of detail, proposals will normally contain the items shown in Exhibit 7.9. In addition there will probably be a statement of the benefits of proceeding. If the proposal is long, or complex, it may be helpful to the reader to put in a summary at the beginning to provide a bird's-eye view of the contents.

A proposal is a selling document, which should persuade the client to use your services in carrying out the project. Supporting evidence (shown in item 9 in Exhibit 7.9) should be tailored to the assignment under consideration. The consultancy therefore must be able to access its relevant experience, particularly if the client wants to take up references. Whether dealing with assignment experience or that of the prospective members of the project team, it should be relevant to the assignment that is under consideration. Standard CVs for consultants are all right as source documents, but they should be tailored for each proposal to highlight the reason an individual consultant is particularly fitted for inclusion on an assignment team.

A proposal should be a manifestation of the value that your consultancy practice can bring to the client. Clients are rarely impressed by general assertions of how wonderful the consultancy practice is.

Nowadays, organisations are rarely embarrassed by using consultants. Presentations made jointly by consultants and client staff at conferences are not

Exhibit 7.9 Contents of a proposal

1. An appraisal of the nature of the client's business, the background of the proposed assignment and the problems to be tackled.
2. Definition of the terms of reference* and scope of the assignment with comments on the validity and any critical aspects of the terms of reference supplied by the client.
3. Proposed approach to the project describing the tasks to be accomplished and the methodology and techniques to be used.
4. A work plan indicating the timetable, sequence and duration of tasks and the total elapsed time needed to complete the assignment.
5. A statement of the expected results and outputs from the assignment.
6. Details of the form and frequency of reporting and arrangements for regular liaison with client staff.
7. Proposed staffing levels and roles to be assigned to consulting staff and client counterpart staff and an estimate of the total time inputs proposed.
8. Fee and expenses quotation and invoicing procedures (which may be presented separately).
9. Supporting information on the consultancy's services, and relevant assignment experience and curricula vitae of the assignment team members.
10. Details of the consultancy's standard terms and conditions (or the terms and conditions applicable to the particular assignment).
11. Methods for assuring the quality of the assignment.

(Source: Institute of Management Consultancy)

(*Note that 'term of reference' is used here in a more conventional sense than is used in this book).

unusual. Nonetheless, references to other clients should be made circumspectly when talking to prospective clients. Bear in mind that prospects will assume that you will discuss them and their business in the same way with your other clients. A client's permission should be sought before discussing with other clients the work you have done for them. From a prospect's view, however, it can be tremendously helpful to talk to an existing client – and a valuable selling aid to a consultancy if given a glowing reference.

The reasons for using your firm should be included in almost every proposal. If the need for the project for which you are proposing is already widely accepted, then you may need to do no more. If, however, the sponsor or some of the sponsor's colleagues have yet to be convinced of the benefit of proceeding, then you should make clear the rationale underlying the project and the benefits of proceeding.

NURSING THE SALE

Once the proposal has been submitted, the sale will need to be nursed. It is rarely satisfactory to submit a proposal and then wait for a 'yes/no' answer.

Ideally the salesperson should know the steps involved in the client's decision making process and be on hand to deal with any difficulties and to direct attention to the benefits of your undertaking the project.

Some organisations have standard processes for the submission of bids. For example on many occasions there is a separation between the technical evaluation of a proposal and its commercial evaluation. Bidders may therefore need to submit two documents: one which describes how they will tackle the project, and a separate pricing document. Clients may also have specified the timetable to be followed after submission. For example, they may have a period during which they might ask questions of clarification, and then a further step where they meet shortlisted bidders to discuss their proposals with them.

However, if there is no pre-specified process that the client wants you to follow, then immediately after submitting the proposal, the salesperson might contact the prospect to:
- check that the proposal has been received;
- get initial reactions and confirm the decision making process;
- identify any real difficulties the client has in choosing your proposal and deal with intrinsic objections.

On this last point, note that in the private sector particularly, price is only one of several factors that influence a client's buying decision.

Classic negotiation on the cost, payment terms and so on may be required, but these are less important than the prospect:
- believing that you have clearly understood their needs;
- having confidence in the consultancy's people;
- believing that the proposed approach will achieve the benefits claimed.

If a client is unhappy with a proposal, therefore, see this as a joint problem solving process. The client needs consultancy, you want to provide it, so how can this be done to the best advantage of all concerned? When a client expresses concern, the salesperson must probe to find out what that concern really is.

For example, suppose your estimate of the consultancy fees for a particular job is £20,000, and the client is resistant to this. Let's assume that your fee estimate is based on a costing of fee days times daily fee rate. An obvious option is to attempt to reduce the fees. If, however, your fee rate is realistic and your estimate of the time required is accurate, then reducing the total fee means changing one of these.

The general practice within consultancy firms is to set fee rates annually (or more frequently during periods of high inflation) at a fixed level for costing purposes. In this environment, this means that a reduction in total fees will show up as a 'loss', i.e. the same number of days at a lower fee rate than standard. The result is that there is then some pressure to do the job more quickly, or to use less expensive resources, both of which are likely to diminish quality.

So, go back to the original problem: why does the client want to reduce the fees? Is it because they do not think it represents value for money? Or is it because they do not have the budget?

If their reservations are about value for money, do you as their consultant truly believe that the benefits of this project adequately outweigh the costs, both actual and opportunity costs? If you do, then the problem is one of communication; the client:

- does not recognise the benefits; or
- does not value the benefits in the same way as you; or
- lacks the confidence that the benefits will accrue.

In these circumstances the salesperson's task is to diagnose which of these applies and then take remedial action.

Of course, if the benefits are not worthwhile, should you be advising them to proceed with the project in the first place?

If the client's problem concerns their budget, can the budget be changed? If the answer is no, the onus is upon you to see what you can do to restructure the project within the time allowed by a reduced budget, usually by reducing the scope. I find an effective strategy is to go through this with the client. We go through the tasks and the estimate of times required for each, to see what can be pared. This allows the client to make suggestions that may not have occurred to me, as well as making clear what the effect of the reduced budget will be.

Treating this as a serious problem, and engaging in joint problem solving with the client, will also help to build a good relationship between you.

LOSING THE SALE

Not every bid will succeed, but don't lose heart! If you have been sufficiently impressive, you should be invited to be on the tender list for the next piece of consultancy that you could do for that client. Anyhow, a good bid should cement the client relationship, and provide the basis for further discussion about what you have to offer in other areas of consultancy.

DEVELOPING SELLING SKILLS

In this section we consider some of the basic skills that are needed in conducting activities in the selling process.

BASIC SKILLS IN SELLING

The danger of being dogmatic over any aspect of selling is that there is almost certainly a salesperson somewhere who, despite breaking any rule you care to mention, is being enormously successful. In many ways, the choice of method of approach is a personal one. Just as the same style of dress would not suit everybody, so too do different sales people have different styles.

'Selling the wheel' (Cox & Stephens) is a parable about the man who invents the wheel and the need for different styles of selling depending on product-market maturity. Product-market maturity is defined according to the complexity of the sale and the buyer's familiarity with the product and the process of buying it (see Exhibit 7.10). This also shows the needs of clients at different levels of maturity.

Exhibit 7.10 Product-market maturity and selling style

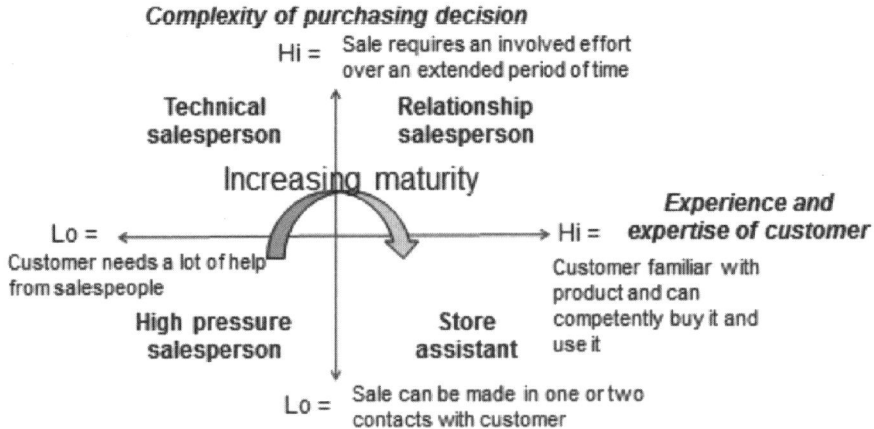

Based on "Selling the wheel", Cox & Stevens

The different styles of selling can be characterised as follows (I have adapted the names they give the different styles):
- The *high pressure salesperson*. This individual is relying on the force of their personality and a powerful style of presentation to make the sale. They are strongly sales orientated.
- The *technical salesperson* depends on their product knowledge to make the sale. Their technique is to take time to understand the client's situation and make recommendations on the technical solution that will help. They are strongly problem orientated.
- The *relationship salesperson* uses the strength of the personal relationship with the client to be a key differentiator in a market

which is becoming commoditised. As their name implies, they regard the relationship with the client as being key.
- The *store assistant* is needed when clients are very clear what they want and all they need is assistance to make the buying process easy. Here the salesperson is strongly product and service orientated and is effectively an order taker.

It is useful to identify which style of selling is the one that you prefer. I would guess that the preferred styles of most consultants are technical or relationship, but these may not be appropriate given a different level of product-market maturity, so it is useful when running a consulting practice to ensure that you have individuals who cover the range of selling styles required by your product portfolio. This is most frequently done when for example firms distinguish between those salespeople who develop sales with new clients versus those who do so with existing clients.

Despite these differences in style, there are many similarities in the skills that all salespeople need.

The initial contact with a prospect is crucial in that it forms the background to the sales activity that follows. Making the initial contact is perhaps one of the most stressful parts of the sales activity for the salesperson. The following tips, therefore, although generally applicable in selling consultancy, should be particularly helpful when approaching a prospect for the first time.
- Listen. We have noted that in consultancy the emphasis is on the prospect specifying what they want and why they want it. You can respond only if you first listen to what they have to say.
- Have a positive vision of your transactions with your prospects. If you expect a successful outcome, you are more likely to achieve it than if you expect to fail. Failure is likely to result if you are about to make a phone call to a prospect and have an internal monologue running that says 'They won't put me through. Even if they do, I'll say all the wrong things. Mr Prospect will ask me all sorts of questions I won't know the answer to...'

Contrast this with a view that says 'I expect to be put through. This will give me the opportunity to have a mutually beneficial discussion with Ms Prospect', etc.

You should therefore aim to begin with a positive rather than negative expectation of the encounter. If it helps, write out the positive scenario on a card. Before making a telephone call or entering a meeting read it to yourself. Gradually the positive attitude should begin to take over.
- In particular, you should have a positive vision of your relationship with the prospect. If you see yourself as a supplicant seeking the

boon of their custom, this will show, and the prospect will treat you as an inferior. The picture you should have in your mind is as fellow professionals with a shared interest – the improvement of the prospect's business.

Of course, you will wish to maintain a professional relationship with your clients on matters to do with work, but this does not imply superiority or inferiority; the client is an expert in their area of work, as you are in yours.

There are clients who want their ego massaged (don't we all to some extent?). If you don't like doing this then, in cases where it is necessary, you must relinquish the client to someone who is good at ego massage!

TELEPHONE SKILLS

The challenge of making a telephone call is that you have no channel from which to get visual data on how the other person is responding. If the call is to someone that you don't know, it is therefore more difficult to strike up a conversation with them than if you meet face to face. My observations from training consultants in this basic skill are:

- When starting the call, smile and perhaps stand. These add energy and friendliness to your voice.
- Slow down at the start of the call. People need to 'tune in' to your voice and will miss information while they are doing so. If you are making a number of calls on the same topic, it is sometimes useful to have a script. Make sure that you use it only as a guide to what you want to say rather than reading it out – it is difficult to sound authentic when reading a script!
- Take your style from that of the person at the other end of the line. If they are brisk and business-like, so should you be; if they are relaxed and friendly, you should match their style.

Even though it is not face to face, the telephone call is a meeting and you need to treat it accordingly.

FACE TO FACE SKILLS

- You will be better able to deal with a meeting effectively if you are calm. I remember attending an initial meeting with an experienced colleague some years ago. We had to climb to the second floor of the office block and I noticed that my colleague was climbing even more

slowly than his senior years required. The reason, he explained, was that he should not reach the client's office out of breath.
- You will be more stressed at the start of a meeting if you are late and you will also create an unfavourable initial impression. The rule is always to arrive in good time with a margin allowed for delays.
- Listen, and show by your body language that you are doing so. Nod encouragingly, ask questions, and take notes. Encourage the other person to talk.

  There will be clients who are verbose or who stray into irrelevancies; bring them back to the topic with a question. You can interrupt without giving offence by saying, 'I wonder if I might interrupt you at this point to ask...?'
- Use non-evaluative or descriptive statements in your questioning, rather than judgmental ones. For example, don't ask, 'Why has your division failed to meet its profit targets?' Better to ask, 'What are the difficulties that have prevented your division meeting its profit targets?' People will more happily admit to difficulties than failure. The trick is to talk of half full bottles rather than half empty ones. (Of course, there are occasions when you will wish to confront a client by using judgmental statements, but this should be by design rather than accident.)
- When questioning, vary the pace. One question rapidly following the last begins to sound like an interrogation. A pause will also serve to show that you are listening.
- Avoid asking double questions; this can be confusing and, most probably you will get answers only to one of the questions. (A double question is of the sort, 'Have things been so difficult in previous years? Do you see an upturn for next year?')
- Another trap is turning open-ended questions into multiple choice close-ended ones. For example, 'How do you see the future prospects for your business? Will competition increase? Or will there be a general recovery in the sector?' The open-ended question has been lost, and the consultant is leading the client.

FRAMING QUESTIONS

Questioning must not, of course, be an interrogation! Happily, however, most people like to talk about their business if asked properly.

As the questioning progresses, you gradually move from the use of non-directive, open-ended questions to directive questions. You may also find that the focus of the questioning changes – for example, from dealing with one small part of the organisation to issues affecting the organisation as a whole.

Use open-ended questions to broaden the discussion. These are the questions that typically begin with Who, What, Why, When, How or Where.

Directive questions are the questions prefaced Would, Could, Should, Will, Is, If, May and Can. They restrict the response to a yes/no answer. They help to check your understanding of the information that has been elicited by the open-ended questions.

In both cases, the pressure of silence may encourage the prospect to open up. What is equally true is that if you are talking, the other person is not. You need to encourage them by your questioning to give you the information you require.

Of course, people will give information in response not only to questions. An assertion or a comment may also elicit a response. Listen to any popular radio or TV news programme to hear examples of these frequently used.

TEAM SELLING

In order to satisfy Wittreich's third criterion, it may be sensible for more than one consultant to attend the sales meeting. Whenever there is more than one consultant attending a meeting with a client, whether it is the first or a subsequent meeting, it is important that you have worked out your respective roles. You should have decided how you are to position yourselves with the client. If the aim is that one of you is to be the leader of the project, if it is sold, then that person must be allowed to establish their credentials with the client.

At the very least, you should decide which of you is to lead the discussion at the meeting. The person who leads should make openings for the other to make a contribution; it doesn't help the selling process to be fighting over air time. It is also incumbent on the person in the secondary role to respond to the openings provided by the leader. Some years ago, I was in a sales role and took along a technical expert to meet a prospect. I kept on making opportunities for him to contribute, passing the conversation over to him with comments like 'Wouldn't you say that was the case?', but he refused to respond. It was like serving tennis balls to someone who made not the slightest effort to return them. Eventually, the prospect got tired of this and asked me 'Who's this then – your pet parrot?' That was the last meeting with that organisation.

DEALING WITH OBJECTIONS

Objections come in two forms:
- *extrinsic*, which are general, to do with using consultants, your firm or you;
- *intrinsic*, which are about the specific details of your proposition.

Extrinsic objections tend to come earlier on in the sales process; if you cannot deal with them satisfactorily then, you will find it difficult to progress. In dealing with them:
- make sure that the objection is not based on a false assumption or misapprehension;
- probe to find out what the real concern is.

Be prepared to handle the most common objections; remember that it is not only the answer itself, but the manner in which it is given that will inspire confidence. So make a checklist of the extrinsic objections that have given the most difficulty, and prepare suitable answers to handle them.

Intrinsic objections give you information about the client's needs that will enable you to refine your proposition. Again, it is worth probing to find out what the real concern is. You need also to make sure you elicit all objections before revising your proposition, and here the 'trial close' is useful.

The trial close is an 'if... then...' statement: 'If we bring the price down to meet your budget, then would you proceed?' is an example. It avoids wasting time satisfying a client's needs only partially when there are other objections to be dealt with.

DEVELOPING SELLING SKILLS

Whether you win or lose a sale, you should carefully analyse the result and apply the lessons to future sales efforts (the process shown in Exhibit 7.11). They may be surprising; for example, many years ago one consultancy won a job and asked, 'Why us?' It emerged that a reason for their success was that they used colour slides in their presentation! The client interpreted the investment in (what was then) more expensive colour as a significant commitment to the project.

Exhibit 7.11 The virtuous circle of improving selling skills

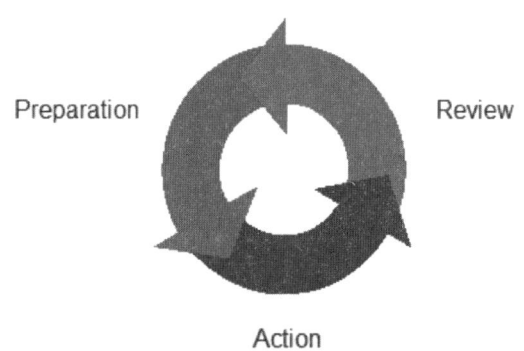

Getting better at selling may mean doing different things or doing things differently. The virtuous circle of improvement shown in Exhibit 7.11 is helpful in thinking about how to do this.

Although the focus in selling is on action, it has to be preceded by careful preparation. After action, you review how things have gone, so that your preparation will be better informed next time. All three steps need to be carried out carefully to improve performance.

At the end of a sales activity which has culminated in putting a proposal to a client, conduct a win/lose review with the client. Find out from them why they selected you, or why you failed to get the contract. Throughout the selling process make it clear that this is something that you intend to do; experienced purchasers of consultancy will expect to do it anyhow. It will yield invaluable information that will help you to develop your selling performance.

8

COMMERCIAL ASPECTS OF CONSULTANCY

If a consultancy firm is to be viable, it must generate revenue. The bulk of income will come from charging fees to clients and so in this chapter we start by considering how these might be determined.

DETERMINING FEE RATES

For the most part the fees charged to a client will be related to the cost of the project, the cost being primarily that of the time spent on it by the consultants in the project team. (Other methods of generating revenue in a consultancy practice are dealt with in a later section.) The cost of the time is usually based on a daily fee rate; the level of fee rate required can be calculated as follows.

At the start of Chapter 6, we considered a consultancy firm which had 25 consultants with a basic pay on average of £40,000 p.a. The fully absorbed on-costs and overheads were assumed to be as much again, resulting in total costs of £2 million p.a. If average utilisation on fees (days on fees divided by paid days) is 60 per cent, the number of fee days in which this has to be recovered is:

60% (utilisation) × 260 (days per year) × 25 (no. of consultants)
= 3900

Break-even fee rate (the fee level required to recover costs) is therefore:
= £2m / 3900
= £513 per day

As the consultancy would also need to make a profit, the budgeted fee rate would need to exceed this, so a budgeted fee rate of, say, £600 per day might be set. This would have to be compared with market rates; if this fee rate is markedly greater, then it may mean that overhead costs have to be reduced, so that the fee rate can be cut.

Consultancies frequently charge different fee rates for different grades of consultant. These can be calculated based on individual salaries, as follows. Using the same example from above, the average annual fee income to be generated by a single consultant is:

60% (utilisation) × 260 (days per year) × £600 (fee rate)
= £93,600 p.a.

The ratio of average fee income to average salary is £93,600/£40,000
= 2.34

In practice, among medium and large sized practices (with larger overheads) this ratio might be twice as much. Someone earning £60,000 p.a. would therefore be expected to generate (2.34 × £60,000 p.a. =) £140,400 revenue, and their fee rate would be set accordingly.

REDUCTIONS IN FEE RATE

There are circumstances when reducing fee rates may be appropriate, such as when a contract offers the opportunity to assign a team of consultants for a long period without interruption. Consultancy managers like large contracts, because:

- as a rule, the cost of selling is a smaller percentage of revenue;
- long projects mean fewer gaps between assignments, when consultants might be not earning fees.

Both these points mean that the utilisation in a consultancy becomes potentially greater when large jobs are being done.

Returning to the example quoted earlier in this chapter: suppose the benefit of changing the sales mix, so that most work consisted of long consultancy assignments, was to increase utilisation from 60 per cent to 65 per cent. The revenue would be increased thus:

Revenue = 65% (utilisation) × 260 (days) × £600 (daily fee rate) ×
25 (number of consultants)
= £2,535,000

This is an increase of about 8 per cent from that where utilisation is 60 per cent. A client, recognising the benefits of a long assignment, may use this as a negotiating ploy to win a reduction in fee rate.

In theory, the consultancy could drop its fee rate by 8 per cent (from £600 per day to £550 per day) and maintain its former revenue. In practice, of course, the decision is rarely arithmetically so precise. The decision to discount will depend on:

- how much you want the work;
- the commercial context – e.g. to prevent a competitor winning the work with a long term, profitable client;
- your relationship with the client;
- what's happening in the rest of the market;
- whether you believe you will lose the assignment if you don't discount.

During a recession, consultancies have been known to discount very heavily to get business. Apart from generating a contribution to fixed costs, the reasons for so doing include:
- wishing to get a toehold in a new client, with the hope of identifying and selling extension work;
- wanting to keep the consultancy team engaged. Consultants need to be kept busy otherwise they become demotivated!

EXPENSES

There are other costs which will come under the heading of expenses, and for which the client will need to budget.

Value added tax (VAT) may need to be added to the bill. This is a matter of little contention when the client is subject to VAT, but will represent a real additional cost if the client cannot set it against the VAT on their own business outputs (as with some public sector organisations).

There may be additional resources needed to be bought in to carry out the assignment. These can include:
- specialist equipment;
- software;
- specialist advice or sub-contractors;
- purchase of licences.

The need for these will depend on the nature of the assignment. On most assignments, however, travel, subsistence and accommodation expenses will be incurred. When an assignment entails travel to a number of locations, particularly if long distances and overnight accommodation are involved, these can quickly mount up. (You also need to consider whether there should be a charge for travel time; whether or not the client pays explicitly for this, the consultant still needs to be paid for this time).

Consultancy practices usually have rules governing travel costs (mileage rate for cars, class of travel by train or plane, use of taxis and hired cars), accommodation (grade of hotel) and subsistence (e.g. a daily rate). These can provide the basis for estimating the likely expenses under this heading. For example, in the week that I write, I have just had to arrange a short interview

programme with a client, which involves travel to locations in London, Bristol and Manchester, and we have agreed a budget as follows:
- London: no charge as close to head office.
- Bristol: travel by car, at an agreed mileage rate.
- Manchester: travel to Heathrow by car; shuttle by air to Manchester; taxi to Manchester centre, and return.

Although this is a trivial example, estimates of expenses on larger jobs can be built up in a similar way.

It is worth establishing what the client's rules are for their own employees incurring expenses. For example, a client may balk at paying for business class flights for consultants when their rules for their own staff require them to travel economy. Indeed, I frequently find that invitations to tender require bidders to agree to expense rules that are set by the client.

There may be other expenses related to in-house costs, such as data processing, administration or material production. For the treatment of these, see below under 'non time-related charges'.

WHAT DO WE TELL THE CLIENT?

Having estimated what the likely costs are on an assignment, what do you agree with the client? The Institute of Management Consultancy provided some helpful guidance:

'There must be a clear understanding between client and consultant:
- *as to the objective of the assignment;*
- *the fees or the basis of fees to be charged.*

So besides defining appropriate terms of reference, a consultant's proposal should quote:
- *a fixed fee, or*
- *a range within which the fee will fall, or,*
- *the fee rate(s) to be charged in terms of time (hour, day, week) or other defined basis, or,*
- *(recruitment work) a percentage of emoluments of appointee (with careful definition as necessary of 'emoluments'), any minimum fee or other conditions.*

When significant expenses are likely to arise for the client's account some explanation or estimate should be given.'

Some contracts are on a 'time and materials' basis: the consultancy keeps a record of the time spent on the assignment, and the related expenses, and charges the client accordingly. The consultant may give an indication of the likely total costs, but is not bound by that. The time and materials basis is used infrequently in management consultancy; it still pertains, however, in other professions e.g. among lawyers on domestic matters.

Most contracts, therefore, are not on a time and materials basis, so you have to tell the client how much the total costs are likely to be to achieve the deliverables required. This estimate is expected to be reasonably binding; the client will not expect you to charge more than the price stated without good cause. The reason for this is simple; most organisations have a budgeting system that requires budget holders to predict likely expenditure. If a manager has authority to spend, say, £30,000 on a consultancy project, it can be politically embarrassing for them to feel obliged to ask for £10,000 more because the consultants had underestimated the cost of the assignment.

One way of avoiding this is to add a 'contingency' to your estimate, e.g. to tell the client to budget for the cost of 20 days fees when you estimate the project will need only 17. This has the advantage that the client will either be charged less, or get more for their money, than expected. (Or, if you are cynical, the consultant will take longer to do the same job, or the consultancy will make more profit!) But even if you add a contingency factor, there is the question, how much should it be? A small contingency will allow for minor errors or alterations to the assignment programme, but will not cover a large misjudgement of the amount of time required. Note that the purpose of a contingency is to cope with underestimates of the amount of work required to carry out a particular project – not to cover changes in the terms of reference.

For the consultancy, therefore, the question is one of managing risk. Furthermore, if there is keen price competition for winning an assignment, the consultancy has to balance the need to keep the price low versus the risk of not allowing enough time to do the work.

This difficulty is compounded when dealing with multi-phase assignments. For example, in the ICC case study (see Chapter 6), John Smith is first going to diagnose what are the major issues leading to high product costs. The next phase will be to address those issues. Although John Smith can estimate with some accuracy the amount of work involved in the first phase, that involved in the next will depend on what he finds out during this diagnosis. It is therefore difficult to estimate how much work would be involved in the second phase before the first is completed. Nonetheless, his client, the General Manager, will probably want an idea of the likely costs of the total project. Not unreasonably so; John Smith might ask for, say, £9,000 to do the first stage of the work, but this is only the start of meeting the client's objective. The GM will want to know what the next stage is likely to cost. Is it going to be £10,000 or £100,000?

So you are faced with a 'Catch 22' situation: you cannot start the work unless you provide an estimate for the whole project, and you cannot provide a precise estimate until you have started the project.

There are several techniques that help to resolve this dilemma.
- Make explicit the assumptions on which your fee estimate is based. If, for example, you are carrying out data collection by interview, then list the locations at which you will be carrying out the interviews and how many people you expect to see at each. If the client then wants you to see more people, or visit other locations, this is a clear departure from the terms of reference, which invites an adjustment to the fee estimate.
- A similar approach can be used for estimating (as yet undefined) future phases of work. You could identify one or two likely scenarios that might emerge after the diagnostic phase, and indicate the consultancy costs that would be involved in dealing with these. Again, if you have made your assumptions explicit, findings that depart from these will provide the basis for amending the fee estimate.
- Quote a fee range. The amount of time required to carry out an assignment is not totally predictable. Telling a client that an assignment will take 21 days implies a degree of precision that is usually spurious. If you say it will take (say) 19 to 23 days, this shows that at this stage it is difficult to be precise. As the assignment progresses, you can tell the client where in this range the out-turn is expected to be.

Even though you surround an estimate with caveats, any figure you quote will be an 'anchor' against which the client will compare any further estimates. Above all, with fees, as with all other aspects of the client relationship, the consultant should manage clients' expectations. 'No surprises' is a good motto.

TERMS OF PAYMENT

The financial structure of a typical consultancy practice is that although revenue is dependent on sales volume, costs are largely fixed. Costs arise mainly from employee costs and office overheads such as premises.

Such a financial structure means that cash flow has to be rigorously controlled. Take, for example, John Smith's practice, where a consultant costs an average of £80,000 p.a. with fully absorbed costs. Assume John Smith starts work on 1 May on a three-month assignment, which is completed satisfactorily on 31 July. If he has worked 62 days at £600 per day in this period, the fees will be £37,200, against costs of £20,000 (being the cost related to three months of his time). The profit of £17,200 is healthy. The cash flow may not be, though. Suppose the consultancy submits an invoice for the fees on 15 August. The client may have a system that pays the invoice at the end of the month following that of submission. This invoice will then be paid on 30 September, and the consultancy receives the amount a few days later. The consultancy has therefore had to bear:

- the cost of an increasing amount of work in progress while the project was being carried out;
- the full cost of the assignment for two months while raising the invoice and waiting for it to be paid.

If this is replicated across the practice, it will need a large amount of working capital, which will add to the costs of the business. It is therefore important to keep work in progress and debtors low, and this starts with the terms of payment, included in the terms of business.

Because of the time lag in the example given above, consultancies like to have payment on account, or interim payments, for an assignment. These will be against the fees agreed, but the fact that they are made before the end of the assignment will help improve cash flow. The aim is to transfer 'work in progress' to 'debtors' quickly.

In an ideal world a client would pay for an assignment on commissioning it. This would be marvellous for the consultancy's cash flow, but bad for the client's. Clients are (for the most part) also subject to the same cash flow considerations as the consultancy firm; from the client's point of view, their cash flow would be considerably enhanced by deferring payment until well after the completion of a consultancy project.

There has to be a compromise. The client might make stage payments throughout an assignment, perhaps at significant milestones. For example, a recruitment consultant might be paid as follows:
- One-third of the fee at the start of the assignment;
- One-third on presentation of a shortlist of candidates;
- One-third on the position being filled.

Whenever there are interim payments, consultants should try to ensure that invoices coincide with the client receiving some value, as in the above example, or on submission of a report, or the completion of a phase of a project.

Fees might also be charged according to the time spent by consultants each month. In the example given above, the invoicing schedule might be as shown in Exhibit 8.1.

Exhibit 8.1 Invoicing schedule

Month	Days on fees	Amount (£) Invoiced
May	19	11,400
June	21	12,600
July	22	13,200
Total	62	37,200

Some firms on major projects might invoice more frequently – perhaps on a weekly basis. Whatever the basis of invoicing, this should be agreed with the client and summarised in the terms of business.

CREDIT TERMS

The other major factor affecting cash flow is the time lapse between the client receiving an invoice and paying it. At the start of my consulting career I was told to find out the payment procedures at a new client and 'train' them to pay the consultancy invoices promptly!

Businesses sometimes have payment systems that classify accounts payable into categories of payment at (say) 7 days, 30 days, 60 days, 90 days. Unless the consultancy insists otherwise, the client will put the account payable into the category that offers maximum credit, so the credit period should be agreed and specified in the terms of business.

Payment can be deferred if there is a query on an invoice. Businesses seeking to improve their cash flow may excuse non-payment because 'We have a query on the invoice', whether or not there are grounds for query. Here the consultancy practice might agree with the client at the outset that queries must be raised within a given time after the invoice has been received, otherwise the invoice will be regarded as acceptable.

A consultancy's own procedures can also result in high levels of working capital being required. For example, in one practice, invoices for the month were raised by the 16th of the following month. These were then sent to consultants for onward transmission to their clients. Because of queries, consultants being out of the office, and this task being given a low priority compared with selling and operating, it often took as long as a further month before the invoices were sent out. This resulted in high levels of work in progress and debtors. The situation was resolved by the invoices being sent out without approval, direct from the accounts department to the client, but on an agreed basis for each assignment.

The final building block in keeping working capital requirements down is credit control. Consultancies should have a system for chasing up invoices due, but not yet paid.

PAYMENT OF A RETAINER

A simple arrangement is where a consultant reserves a number of days in a period for a client, in exchange for which the client will pay a retainer. If the client does not take the days, then the retainer is still payable. If the client wants more time than the contracted amount, this is subject to negotiation.

This can help guarantee a base load of work and improve cash flow if the retainer is payable in advance.

Suppose in the ICC case study (Chapter 2), the GM decides that he would like John Smith's services on average for one day per month, not to carry out a specific project, but to provide general advice and counsel. The GM might pay John Smith a retainer for a year of 12 days' fees. There would be rules about John Smith's availability – for example, it would not be in the spirit of the retainer for the GM to take nothing for the first 11 months and insist on 12 days in the twelfth. The rule might therefore be 'up to two days in any one month, and up to six days per quarter; a maximum of 12 days in any one year, additional days to be subject to negotiation'.

Retainers are attractive to a consultancy firm, as they represent a guaranteed fixed base workload. Their usefulness to clients, however, is of limited value. Circumstances where they might be applied by clients are:

- with a technical specialist.
- to secure exclusive services (i.e. to prevent the client's direct competitors having access to the specialist).
- to secure consultancy services that are not project based (e.g. where a consultant might be used in a temporary, part-time, executive role by a client).

A consultancy practice might also use retainers to secure the services of key sub-contractors.

CANCELLATION CHARGES

A consultancy can incur expense if a project is cancelled or postponed by a client, particularly at short notice. For example, if a consultancy has reserved two consultants to run a three-day interview programme next week, which the client then postpones, it is usually difficult to find fee-earning work at such short notice to fill their time. Even if the consultancy work is carried out at a later date, the six consultant-days next week will have been lost.

Under these circumstances, a consultancy practice may seek redress by having a cancellation clause in the contract. This is particularly appropriate when running short projects or training courses, which tend to be once-off events. Obviously whether the cancellation charge is levied will be subject to wider considerations of the client relationship. Part of the value of a cancellation or postponement clause is, however, that it can deter clients from changing a programme needlessly – it becomes more worthwhile for them to put themselves out to avoid the cancellation charge!

OTHER METHODS OF GENERATING REVENUE IN CONSULTANCY

For the most part, revenue is generated by fees, which are related to the time spent on a project but if all income is time related, then once you have established your fee rate, there is a theoretical maximum revenue you can get. So a perennial concern in a consultancy practice is the creation of non time-related income.

If the revenue is to be increased without taking on more employees, the options are:
- to increase the fee rate;
- to increase the utilisation.

My experience of fee rates is that price is rarely the major determinant in the choice of consultant. Other factors being equal, clients will choose the consultancy quoting the lowest fees; the consultancy firms quoting, however, will attempt to ensure that other factors are not equal, but seek to impress through their grasp of the client's problem and the quality of their people. This leads to some tolerance of difference in fee rate; a client would rather pay £50,000 for a consultancy with whom they were keen to work than £45,000 where the results are expected to be indifferent.

So some increase in fee rate might be possible. There will be a market rate and it may be possible to command a premium; even so, this is unlikely to be much above 10–20 per cent.

The alternative method of increasing revenue is to increase utilisation. Again, here there is an upper limit to the number of fee days. Once time has been allowed for annual and statutory holidays, say 35 days p.a., the number of working days available is down to 225 per person. Out of this, time has to be allowed for:
- sales and marketing;
- product development;
- administration;
- training courses and conferences;
- sickness.

The time spent on each of these will be distributed unevenly across the practice; some consultants will do little other than operating on fees. Others may spend their time primarily on selling (see Exhibit 6.5 for examples of the budgets for consultants with different roles). The point is that it is difficult to raise utilisation to an average of more than 80 per cent without harm in the long term to the practice. Important tasks would be neglected. In practice, too, assignments do not fit neatly together – there are delays to their starting, which means that there is often waiting time for an individual consultant between assignments.

So the control of fee rate and utilisation offers only limited opportunities for increasing revenue. Consultancy managements usually ensure that there are tight controls on utilisation; it is monitored frequently (often weekly) and forecasted so that scheduling can be adjusted accordingly. Fee rates are regularly reviewed, too, so the scope to increase utilisation and fee rate is limited in a well-managed practice. If the productivity of existing resources is optimised, how else can revenue be increased?

DECOUPLING PRICE AND COST

Professionals typically charge a standard fee rate, irrespective of the value of the work they do, but occasionally the fee can be related to the value of the work — for example:
- In mergers and acquisition work, a successful transaction is of considerable value to the parties involved. Professional advisers may relate their fees to the value of the transaction.
- In recruitment work, the fees may be related to the emoluments of the appointed candidate.

Sometimes fees will be success-related. For example, again in recruitment, at least part of the fee will be conditional on finding a suitable candidate to fill the vacancy. There have also been consultancies which, in their corporate development work, have accepted an equity stake in the company as part payment of their fees.

In theory, consultancies might also receive payment based on the benefits that their assignment has produced – i.e. performance related fees. There are arguments against this when:
- It can be difficult to produce a satisfactory base case.
- It may influence the consultants to produce recommendations biased towards optimising their fees rather than the client's business performance.
- Changes may not be the result of the consultancy project (e.g. reduced costs can result from a decrease in business activity instead of improved performance).
- Improvements may depend on the performance of client staff as well as the efficiency of the consultancy project.
- There will be a long wait for the consultancy to be paid if the benefits might accrue only over a long period of time.

If these points can be satisfactorily addressed, the consultancy charge might be based on the share of the benefits. Some professional organisations of which consultants are members may prohibit this basis of fees, and so this should also be checked.

USING SUB-CONTRACTORS

Sub-contractors are usually paid only for the time they spend on fee earning work. This generates a contribution, being the difference between their daily fee rate and the rate that the client is paying. The related overhead is usually small. Sub-contracting has the further benefits that:
- it introduces some variability in the cost base. If the volume of sales decreases, you can reduce the amount of work sub-contracted before you have to consider cutting staff.
- sub-contractors can be used to bring skills that are not available elsewhere in the consultancy.

The disadvantages of sub-contracting are that sub-contractors:
- may not be available when you want them, being engaged on projects for other principals.
- are not subject to the same control as full-time employees. This may present difficulties in enforcing a uniformity of approach and standard of quality.
- yield less profit than full-time staff.

The indications are, however, that consultancies are moving the same way as their clients, in that they use sub-contractors increasingly. Indeed, some clients are now insisting that, although overall responsibility for a major project may be given to a large practice, they would expect to see elements of it given to specialist sub-contractors and – in some major projects – the work to be conducted by a consortium. This is because it is unlikely that the best consultants or expertise for all elements needed in a project are in a single practice or, indeed, that the work involved is restricted to consultancy.

NON-TIME RELATED CHARGES

Consultancy practices can generate income by charging for items related to an assignment, other than the time spent on it. Items that might be charged in such a way include:
- proprietary software;
- use of a proprietary methodology;
- use of psychometric tests and other survey instruments;
- results of research (e.g. market research survey) and other proprietary data;
- organising conferences or training that the client attends.

For the most part, these represent income from the sale of intellectual property. The consultancy will have invested time and effort in creating the item (or it may have bought a licence from someone who has done so) and is monetising this.

Sometimes a firm will make a standard charge of a percentage of the fee for 'administration, telephone calls, etc'. This will only approximate to the actual cost, but obviously involves less work than monitoring and costing every administrative expense. The basis of charging expenses should be clear to clients. The danger in making a standard charge is where it is part of the terms of business, which the client has not read properly, so that the first they learn about it is when it appears on an invoice from the consultancy.

I have to confess to a personal dislike of this basis of charging for administrative and office expenses; I believe the fee rate should cover all routine costs, with additional charges being made only for exceptional costs on an agreed basis. For example, a consultancy might charge for producing a specialist e-learning package to support a project.

TERMS OF BUSINESS

The commercial aspects of the client relationship are embodied in a practice's Terms of Business. Unlike Terms of Reference, which are usually designed for each client project, Terms of Business are likely to be similar for different projects. Thus far in this chapter, we have considered only the basis of payments made by the client to the consultancy, but there will be other matters that might be routinely included in Terms of Business, such as:
- intellectual property rights;
- conditions affecting the liability of the consultancy;
- expectations of what the client is to provide;
- other contractual terms, such as how the assignment may be terminated before its completion.

A consultancy practice may have standard Terms of Business that are included in each proposal, with variations, or optional clauses, which are tailored to a particular contract.

INTELLECTUAL PROPERTY RIGHTS

With the growth of the 'knowledge economy', intellectual property rights (IPR) are of increasing importance. This is particularly the case in consultancy, where – presumably – consultants are hired because of their know-how. It is the exercise of this intellectual property that clients are buying, and it would be difficult for a client justifiably to insist that a consultant's know-how became the client's own intellectual property.

IPR becomes a particular issue in matters of specific intellectual property generated on a project, for which a client might reasonably suppose they have paid. This might include, for example:
- product design;
- software development;
- operational processes.

What in theory might happen, for instance, is that a consultancy is paid six months' fees for developing a piece of software for a client A. Another client, B, needs similar software, which would cost six months' fees again, but the consultancy could sell the software developed for Client A. Maybe it might need a month's worth of adjustment, but the consultancy could sell it for five months' fees. Client B would be happy because they have got their software at a discount, and the consultancy would be happy because they have got five month's revenue for one month's effort. On the other hand, Client A may be less happy at funding this!

Of course, this is a feature of consultancy: consultants acquire learning and experience with clients, which is then deployed to the benefit of later clients. The most that clients can do to protect their interests in this situation is to agree a restriction on future work with direct competitors (see 'clients' terms of engagement', below). Where intellectual property is developed as a specific product of a project however, the rights to this should be agreed as part of the Terms of Business. This, of course, equally applies to the consultancy's intellectual property provided to the client, who may be subject to restrictions on its use.

THE LIABILITY OF THE CONSULTANCY

In the same way as it is unwise to enter marriage with a divorce settlement in mind, you should never start any consultancy project contemplating its failure. Even so, there are risks associated with all consultancy work, and it is important to have thought through the arrangements if things do not work out as expected.

Although there have been a few court cases in which major practices have been sued, these are exceptional. It is important to have an 'escalation' rather than a 'tripwire' strategy (to use phrases from the Cold War!) In other words, there should be a series of measures in which consultancy and client can engage before resorting to the courts, which is rarely to commercial benefit, although it may apportion blame.

It therefore makes sense to have some form of dispute resolution procedure. In my experience disputes tend to be about misunderstandings rather than breaches of contract, both parties being convinced of rather different things. This reinforces the importance of establishing clear Terms of Reference at the start, and maintaining effective communications with the client (and documenting agreements) throughout the project.

EXPECTATIONS OF WHAT THE CLIENT IS TO PROVIDE

Consultancy projects are joint ventures between the consultancy and the client, and it is rare for the client's contribution to be limited simply to funding. The client's staff will be involved and their time and co-operation will usually be critical to success. In addition there may be other obligations on what the client is to provide, which may be incorporated within the Terms of Business, such as:
- office accommodation and facilities (e.g. access to Wi-Fi);
- administrative support;
- logistical help (e.g. booking flights, accommodation);
- provision of information.

The detailed nature of these will vary according to the type of work being carried out. For example, in running in-house training courses, a consultancy would want to establish responsibility for:
- making administrative arrangements for participants to attend;
- booking the training venue;
- providing copies of training materials;
- hiring equipment.

OTHER CONTRACTUAL TERMS

Other contractual terms might include:
- The basis on which fees might be varied. For example, in a time of high inflation, a consultancy might wish to review fee rates during the course of a long project.
- *Client confidentiality.* This is usually a matter of ethics, and an aspect of each operating consultant's personal contract of engagement. Strictly, it should be superfluous, but clients often take comfort from the confirmation that these arrangements are explicit.
- *Early termination of contract.* There may be circumstances in which a project is rendered no longer necessary, or other occasions in which a client wishes to terminate a contract, or a booking. Cancellation

and termination terms should be clear. From the consultancy's side, they will have promised to make the designated consultants available for the required time, and hence the consultants cannot be assigned to alternative pieces of work on which they might be deployed. Cancellation or termination at short notice may mean that it is not possible to find alternative work. Some penalty is usually agreed beforehand; for example, a training business might insist on full payment if a bespoke training course is cancelled within two weeks of it being due to run. This type of penalty means that clients make cancellations only for serious reasons.

There may be other contractual terms to be placed in your Terms of Business. Sometimes, however, clients will have their own views of the Terms of Engagement for consultants.

CLIENTS' TERMS OF ENGAGEMENT

Companies that are frequent users of consultants may themselves have a standard form of consultancy contract they use and this is especially the case when their purchasing departments are involved. This will cover much the same ground as the Terms of Business of the consultancy practice, but be orientated to the needs of the client rather than the consultancy. I have been subject to these from time to time, and the points of interest in one such are as follows:

- The client reserves the right to ask for replacement of a consultant if in their opinion the performance of the consultant is unsatisfactory;
- Consultants working on the project are subject to approval by the client, approval being based on the consultants' CVs and interview;
- The consultancy should keep records of all activities undertaken on the project, and make them available to the client if so requested;
- The consultancy must show appropriate levels of Public Liability and Professional Indemnity insurance;
- There are terms affecting intellectual property rights;
- There are clauses relating to non-solicitation (i.e. not poaching the client's employees) and working for the client's direct competitors for a period after the end of the contract.

These topics are ones that relate to all consultancy projects, and therefore can be fairly included as part of the contract. What the consultancy has to do in each case is to decide whether the terms are reasonable. Clients' purchasing departments are likely to have a standard form of contract that they will send to you for agreement. It is then up to you to negotiate any variation to the details with the purchasing department.

9
MANAGING A CONSULTANCY BUSINESS

As with any other business, a management consultancy has to be managed and, if only in the long term, the quality of management will influence the performance of the business. It is not the purpose of this book to rehearse the general principles of management; it is useful, however, to consider the critical elements that need to be managed.

A useful general model of key elements in a consultancy practice is illustrated in Exhibit 9.1.

Exhibit 9.1 A model of a consultancy practice

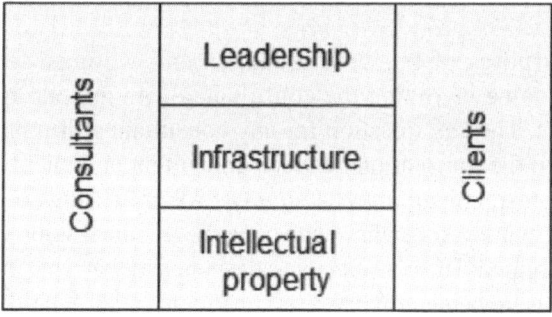

The model shows that the function of a consultancy organisation is to enable consultants and clients to add value to each other through harnessing the leadership, infrastructure and intellectual property of the consultancy practice. These are covered below, together with some of the demands on managing consultants and concluding with some of the challenges involved in managing a consultancy highlighted in the model in Exhibit 9.1.

LEADERSHIP IN A CONSULTANCY PRACTICE

I seem to remember from the days when I was taught corporate strategy that the first question to ask when fashioning a strategy is, 'What business are we in?' Perhaps strategic thinking has moved on since then but it is a good question to ask of a consultancy business.

Large consultancy practices have taken to adding a strapline to all their publicity material, which is the answer to this question. This is usually to the effect, 'Helping our clients to become more successful.' But how is this to be done?

Consultancies add value to their clients through the medium of their consultants. Exhibit 9.2 shows a model of a consulting practice, expressed as exchanges of value between consultancy firm, consultant and client.

Exhibit 9.2 An added value model of consultancy

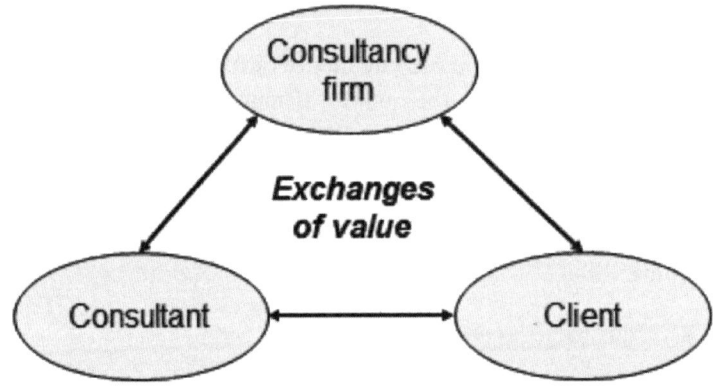

For the purposes of business management, we need to consider the exchanges of value involving the consultancy firm at both operational and strategic levels. The key question for any consultancy firm is, 'What do we as a firm add to the transaction between consultant and client?'

At its simplest, consultancy is simply brokerage: the consultancy firm introduces its clients to specialists who have the technical skills needed to carry out the work required. The consultant has the benefit of carrying their employer's franchise – they are being employed as consultants at least partly because they bear the imprimatur of their employer. The client has the reassurance of the reputation of the practice underwriting the work of the individual consultants, which provides a greater sense of security; employing consultants is thereby not only outsourcing work but also risk. The practice makes a profit on the difference between what they charge the client and what they pay the consultant.

The thought will occur eventually to both client and consultant that it might be to the advantage of both to cut out the intermediary – the consultancy firm.

A sole practitioner is the result of this thinking taken to its logical conclusion. Nonetheless there is a role for a broker between clients and consultants but this is more often the function of networks or associations than that of a consultancy practice. So a consultancy firm has to offer something more in the long term.

ORGANISATION STRUCTURE WITHIN A CONSULTANCY PRACTICE

Like other industries, many forms of organisation have been tried out in consultancy:
- Industry focused groups;
- Consultants grouped by specialisation;
- Regional groups, concentrated by geography;
- A combination of some or all of the above.

There is no one right answer. Form should follow function, and so organisation structure should be an element of infrastructure that improves the ability of a consultancy practice to enhance its key processes.

CAREER PROGRESSION AND ROLES IN A CONSULTING PRACTICE

Typically the point of entry into a consultancy is as a delivery consultant. With increasing experience you may then progress to having commercial responsibilities for sales and clients. Ultimately you may have a management role in the practice, being responsible for a line of business and bottom line performance.

The population reduces at each level; there are more consultants involved in delivery than in selling, and more involved in selling than management. Some practices operate an 'up or out' policy – either you get promoted or you leave the practice. This has advantages to both the practice and the consultant:
- The practice benefits from a network of (we hope) positively disposed alumni; it can talent spot among delivery consultants to see who might be promoted; and it avoids a cohort of consultants with increasing salary expectations who have ceased to increase their added value to the firm.
- The consultant benefits from having a very clear prospectus for their future with the firm.

More senior roles are not always filled by internal promotion of course. A well connected industry expert might be recruited to help develop sales in a particular sector, or a senior partner from one practice poached from another to take up a management role.

There are exceptions to the up or out policy, of course – for example with deep technical specialists who are of most value continuing in their specialisation rather than taking a different role. And it is not unusual in a consulting practice for rank and role to be decoupled, so a deep technical specialist may enjoy the same (or better!) rewards than a senior manager in a firm.

Finally, these are not mutually exclusive roles: a sales consultant may still be involved in delivery, while a practice manager may still have some delivery and selling responsibilities.

Let's now look at the roles in more detail.

OPERATING CONSULTANT (DELIVERY ROLE)

This is the default role and as mentioned above, even the most senior individual within a firm may do work with a client, although practice management and account management tasks may consume most of their time. Operating consultants may also have responsibilities for identifying new sales opportunities within the clients for whom they are currently working.

PROJECT MANAGER (DELIVERY ROLE)

The job of the consultancy project manager is to meet the project objectives, within the allocated resources, while maintaining good relationships with client staff. If there is only one consultant involved with the project, they have to take the role of project manager, but in larger projects the project manager will be supervising the work of other consultants and may therefore be a more experienced consultant.

Project management however does not imply seniority (remember the decoupling of rank and role mentioned above), so for example, A might supervise B on one project, whereas on another, B might supervise A.

ACCOUNT MANAGER/SALESPERSON (COMMERCIAL ROLE)

As consultants derive much of their revenue from past clients, the role of the account manager is to maintain links with (specified) past and present clients, and may also be responsible for winning business from new ones. The account manager may have a specialisation as a consultant but frequently this may not be relevant to the client's current needs. Other consultants will therefore be engaged in projects for the account manager's clients. But when the project is complete, the project team will move on to other assignments for other clients and the account manager will be left to maintain the client relationship. In this respect, the account manager is a bridge between consultancy and client and the various sales are the vehicles passing over the bridge. Even when there is no traffic, the bridge exists; if there is no bridge, there can be no traffic. So, the relationship must be maintained, even when there are no current projects.

Thus, while the practice manager (see below) sets the commercial context for the project from the firm's point of view, the account manager will be managing the context of the project from a client relationship point of view.

BID MANAGER (COMMERCIAL ROLE)

A bid, or proposal, for a piece of consultancy work might simply involve a short email. If the project is to be of any size, however, it will involve devoting some time and effort to preparing a proposal, which is a project in itself.

In some practices, this is formally recognised by the appointment of a bid manager. The task of the bid manager is to define the terms of reference for the project, to prescribe the methodology, to assess the resources required to carry it out and to prepare a costing of them. It may also involve assessing the risks associated with the project and, where these are felt to be substantial, seeking authority to proceed with putting in the bid.

Usually the account manager or the project manager who is going to work on the project will take this role. Occasionally, however, there may be people whose specialisation is preparing proposals on specific topics. They may also have superior skills and experience in negotiating. This is particularly useful when a client also has a negotiating team separate from the individuals commissioning the project.

PRACTICE MANAGER (MANAGEMENT ROLE)

The role of practice manager is to manage the business of the consultancy practice, or a part thereof. This is a general management role, with responsibility for producing a profit stream.

The survival and profitability of a consultancy's business are superordinate objectives. The practice manager therefore usually has the greatest seniority within a consultancy unit. At an operational level they will be setting priorities and targets and resolving questions of conflict between others in the consultancy unit, e.g. over competition for resources. The practice manager therefore sets the (internal) commercial environment in which consultancy projects are conducted.

The practice manager will also be responsible for setting strategy for their unit, within that for the practice as a whole.

RESOURCE MANAGER (MANAGEMENT ROLE)

It is unusual for consultants to be permanently allocated to a single account. The task of resource management is to deploy consultants among accounts and projects, and to ensure that their utilisation is optimised. Consultants might be allocated to groups for the purposes of resource management according to location or specialisation. Resource managers may also act as 'product champions', with the aim of promoting their specialist services among the internal connectors – account managers – and thence to the consultancy's client base.

AUDITOR (MANAGEMENT ROLE)

The job of auditor is sometimes called quality manager or quality assurance director. The purpose of the role is to monitor projects against quality standards and to design and carry out procedures to ensure that suitable quality standards are established and maintained.

Quality control is not simply a policing function but something that provides a real commercial and competitive advantage. The purpose of the auditor is to provide someone outside the sales and operating teams involved with the sale or delivery of a particular project, who can helpfully comment on how well these tasks are being carried out.

An auditor might carry out inspections of bids or projects to see that they conform to good practice. Inspections can be conducted after a bid is won or lost, at the conclusion of a project or sometime after the end of a project. The auditor can also be a source of counsel and advice during the project.

This does not have to be a full-time role; for example, a consultant in division A of a business can act as auditor for projects in Division B and vice versa.

INTELLECTUAL PROPERTY IN A CONSULTANCY PRACTICE

Know-how (knowledge, skill and experience) is the principal resource that the consultancy firm offers its clients. Technology transfer is the firm's ability to apply these to the benefit of its clients.

The reason an organisation might turn to a firm for help is for the resources that it offers. The firm may be employed because:
- it has knowledge that the organisation does not have;
- although the organisation has the knowledge, it does not have as much experience in applying it as the firm does, or needs the objective view of an outsider;
- although the organisation has the knowledge and experience, it does not have them sufficiently available to engage in the project.

A consultancy firm therefore needs to ensure that it has the resources (in terms of the skill mix and volume) required to meet the needs of organisations in its marketplace. These needs are, of course, changing and so a firm should aim to have the knowledge and experience required to meet these evolving needs as they change with time through selective recruitment, training and development.

Several points merit consideration concerning technology transfer:
- A firm should not only operate in responsive mode; it should alert its clients to opportunities and needs of which the clients may otherwise be unaware. To this end, a firm should be 'horizon scanning' continually. Sometimes a large practice might have an advisory board or panel to help with this made up partly of outsiders, such as academics, business people, politicians and civil servants. They would alert the firm to trends, opportunities and innovations, which might affect the firm's clientele and its own business. Even without an advisory panel, the consultancy business management should make sure that horizon scanning is done regularly.
- The firm should be able to put together its knowledge and experience in ways that are attractive to its clients (this is product and market development). (This does not mean that consultancy offerings are unilaterally the work of the consultancy firm; they may result from strategic alliances with other firms or individuals.) They should be put forward as offering synergy between firm and client and, perhaps, even developed jointly with the client. There has to be some basis for a discussion to start, however, and the firm should take the initiative on this.
- The firm must deliver its knowledge and experience to its clients effectively. This means that individual consultants must be able to work in a client environment. Collectively, the firm must offer both operating methodologies that ease technology transfer and the ability to put together teams of consultants who can work together effectively.

This last point is important. The consultancy firm's know-how consists not only of the knowledge that it deploys to the benefit of its clients, but also skills in deploying that knowledge. These skills result from experience – experience that belongs to individual consultants within the firm.

A key process, therefore, is capturing individual learning and making it corporately available. This can be embodied in standard procedures or guidelines. Knowledge acquisition and diffusion processes are hence an important component of corporate performance.

These require the investment of time and effort. At the simplest level, they require consultant teams to undertake project reviews and to capture and disseminate the lessons learned. Unless this is enforced as a formal discipline, consultants often prefer to move on to the next project with no pause for reflection, and the opportunity for organisational learning is lost.

It is only in recent years that knowledge management has gained widespread attention, but this is perhaps the most helpful paradigm for a consultancy firm. A consulting firm should have processes that enhance this acquisition and distribution of know-how to the benefit of consultants and clients.

MANAGING CONSULTANTS

THE 'MAKE OR BUY' DECISION

As with any other business, a consultancy is faced with a 'make or buy' decision. The major elements of expense are likely to be salaries and office accommodation. There will be other expenses, some of which are directly recoverable from clients, and the development and maintenance of a support infrastructure, but salaries are likely to be the biggest element of expense. The costs in a consultancy practice are therefore mainly fixed. (This was vividly illustrated in one consultancy firm that made about 10 per cent profit; 'Our profit each week is earned only on Friday afternoon,' I was told.)

If costs are to be made more variable, therefore, the consultancy firm has to consider whether to employ people or take them on only on a project by project basis, as sub-contractors or associates. The greater expense arising is compensated by the fact that in recessionary times sub-contractors can be laid off, while the core team of consultants remains intact. Other considerations in using sub-contractors include:

- How should they be badged? Should the client be told that they are subcontractors?
- Will key learning and experience of value to the consultancy practice be lost by using sub-contractors?
- How will sub-contractors be integrated into the project team? If the consultancy operates a particular methodology, will the sub-contractor be able to operate within it? Does the consultancy add value to the subcontractor's services or is it simply acting as a broker?

This last question relates to the level of investment a consultancy practice makes in each of its sub-contractors. If they are trained in the consultancy's methodology, this represents an expense and a possible dilution of the practice's differentiation through its methodology.

What some firms do is to keep in contact with their 'alumni' – consultants who, having been trained by the firm, have left to form their own practices. They are therefore able to form a pool of trained resource that can be called on when required.

REMUNERATION

The cost of consultants is also related to remuneration policy.

Consultancy practices are not exempt from the general rules governing remuneration, i.e. that the fairness of a consultant's remuneration package will be judged by:
- external comparisons (what they might earn if they performed a similar job elsewhere);
- internal comparisons (their remuneration in relation to that of others in the practice).

Where consultancy differs from many other employments is in the career patterns of employees. Often people who enter consultancy plan to spend only part of their careers within the profession, say four to five years, before moving on to further employment as executives in businesses other than consultancy. There is thus a higher staff turnover rate at junior levels in a practice than at senior levels, the latter being populated primarily by those who have chosen to make their career in consultancy.

This pattern of staff turnover has the advantages that:
- it enables new people with fresh ideas to be brought into the firm;
- those who leave will do so with (we hope) a fund of goodwill towards their former employer, and become clients in their new role.

What this means is that there are two classes of employee in a consultancy practice:
1. Those who are doing a job as a stepping stone to something else.
2. Those who see consultancy as a career.

Most people entering consultancy start in the first category and there is thus a transition point when they move into the second. It is important that both the consultancy firm and the individual consultant share the same view of which category the consultant is in. Misapprehensions on either side will result in disappointment. What some consultancy firms do, therefore, is to have career reviews with consultants at significant points in their careers at – say – intervals of three to five years. These reviews check the individual's career aspirations and potential and plan how they can be best met within the practice, or whether a move outside would be better.

The relevance of this to pay is that it points to different pay policies for the two categories.

The pay package for those in category 1 above will consist of primarily short-term elements, e.g. basic pay, profit sharing bonus, and perhaps some immediate benefits in kind. That for those in category 2 will, in addition, have long-term elements, such as pension and stock options or another form of capital appreciation plan. This distinction is perhaps most recognisable in firms which are partnerships, where being made a partner of the firm has traditionally been an indicator of being offered a long-term career.

At an operational level, pay is significant because, as a large fixed expense, it can create problems:
- in cash flow. The firm has to pay the consultant before the client pays the firm.
- in volume sensitivity. If fee revenue goes down, the firm still has to pay the same salary bill.

Actions that can be taken to deal with these are as follows:
- Defer payment by paying salaries later in arrears. This will provide a (once-off) reduction in cash requirements.
- Defer payment by paying a low monthly salary, but adding an annual supplement (a bonus) that brings it up to market rate.
- Relate the size of the bonus to business profitability. This will make salary a partially variable cost; when profits are low, bonus will be smaller, thereby reducing employee costs.

Obviously any action on pay must take into account market practice and the probable response of the consultants to the changes proposed.

ATTRACTING AND RETAINING TALENTED PEOPLE

In the same way that they compete for clients, consultancy practices compete for talent. Often they are seeking recruits with similar backgrounds, abilities and experience and, for the most part, talented people are in short supply. Consultancy practices have therefore to consider how they market themselves to prospective recruits, and how to continue to offer an attractive prospectus to their own consultants.

Employment conditions have to be right, but beyond this a key element of the prospectus for existing and prospective employees is the opportunities for personal growth – the value added to individual employability by working in a particular practice.

Consultants wish to practise, maintain, refresh, and increase their technical skills. This they can achieve in part by working on consultancy projects. They will also need to keep their technical skills up to date by attending appropriate courses and conferences, reading specialist literature and so on. Besides technical skills, however, they need to know:
- how to deliver their skills in a client environment;
- how to effect change in organisations as a consultant.

Many people learn their technical skills as an employee and have learned how to discharge them as such. Working in a client environment as a consultant is different in respect of the commercial environment, the needs for marketing, selling and client care, and the importance of project management. Many topics covered in this book, for example, would therefore be irrelevant to the specialist employee.

A management consultant is also an agent of change. If consultants are to fulfil this role effectively, they must understand the pathology of organisations so that they can interact with them to achieve change.

There are therefore specific consultancy skills to be added to the specialist expertise of a new consultant. To a large extent, consultancy is a craft: skill has to develop through practical experience as much, if not more, than through formal training. Every consultancy business can therefore provide at least the practical part of the training component. Whether it provides formal training may be a function of size. The reasons for training consultants are:
- training may be needed to bring new staff to the standards of operating required;
- training may be needed to maintain and develop the skills of experienced consultants;
- new skills can be imparted and developed by training;
- offering structured approaches to personal development may help the practice to attract and retain good quality staff.

Given that consultancy is a craft skill, the apprenticeship model is a helpful one in developing skills on the job. Skilled consultants can supervise or act as mentors to those less experienced. In the early stages of a consultant's career, they may keep a log of activities in which they have been engaged. Their project work could then be selected to fill in gaps in experience, extending their skills, or improving in areas of weakness.

The individual consultant gains much by working on client projects. Personal development occurs not only through the development activities organised by the consultancy firm, but also through the consultant's assignment experience.

A benefit of working for a consultancy practice is that it enables you to grow your expertise. Under the umbrella of the firm, you may work in a project team in which you can learn as much, if not more, than you contribute. Personal development is therefore helped at an operational level by assigning consultants to projects that help them to grow. This is something more difficult to do as a sole practitioner, where clients employ you in the centre of your expertise, and there is less scope for working in areas where you have little previous experience.

CHALLENGES IN MANAGING A CONSULTANCY PRACTICE

Exhibit 9.1 can serve to illustrate some of the challenges involved in managing a consulting practice by considering the interface between each of the core components with clients and consultants respectively. These can provide a useful checklist as shown in the table below.

Table 9.1 Challenges in managing a consulting practice

Between Leadership and:	
Clients	The value proposition challenge, What exactly should the value propositions be that we sell to our clients and how do we organise ourselves best to deliver them?
Consultants	The talent retention challenge. Consultancy businesses compete for talent as much as they do for clients. Recent research shows that job mobility and job commitment are not the same. Opportunities for personal growth and the sense of belonging in a small group are crucial in supporting commitment. The difficulties for consultancies in creating commitment are compounded when consultants work regularly on client sites, when there is a real risk of alienation from their employer unless some firm action is taken.
Between Infrastructure and:	
Clients	The engagement challenge, How do we organise ourselves best for account management – both in selling and delivering to our clients? There is an inherent conflict between the commercial demands of a consulting practice and the needs of a client (see Chapter 4) and so management structure and processes need to be designed to mitigate this.
Consultants	The performance management challenge. Consultancies need a different scorecard from other businesses.
	Individual consultants are the means by which value is added by the consultancy to its clients and they too need varying methods of being managed. For example, time is the consultant's stock in trade and so needs to be controlled (and all professionals tend to resent the processes involved!) while at the same time they need time to express their innovative and relationship abilities.

	Between Intellectual Property and:
Clients	The branding challenge, which can be simply phrased 'What exactly do you want to be famous for?'
	The market value of a knowledge-based business primarily lies in the quality of its portfolio – the mix of propositions, capabilities and client relationships that keeps a company one step ahead of its competitors. It therefore makes sense to examine its components regularly and make adjustments to:
	• the mix of propositions, where we can distinguish developing new intellectual property from capitalising on, and commoditising it
	• the mix of relationships: input-based, output-based and shared risk arrangements.
Consultants	The consultancy process challenge. How can you best make the knowledge and experience of individual consultants corporately available?
	It is critical to the success of any consultancy business that professional service deliverers learn from each other and from the experience that has been accumulated in the organisation. There thus needs to be some means of capturing this experience.
	You can spend a lot of time and money developing a knowledge management system, but developing some standard consultancy procedures based on the experience of practitioners in the business is the most powerful way of starting to leverage existing expertise.

Well established management consulting practices will have considered and addressed these challenges. But increasingly there are organisations whose main business is not consultancy but which are adding consultancy to their product mix – perhaps to monetise their knowhow, or to penetrate their client's decision making processes more effectively. The challenges for these organisations are amplified as they need to address them within the context of the rest of the 'business as usual'.

EPILOGUE

Most of my career over the last 40 years has been spent in the world of consultancy and so it seems fitting to close with some brief personal reflections based on this experience, which I hope will be helpful to management consultants using this book.

Perhaps the greatest innovation over this period has been the internet, which has provided rapid access to information and thereby saving enormous amounts of time. For example, 40 years ago we used printed directories to find target clients, and when meeting a new client for the first time, information about their business and its performance was available only through libraries. So searching for information took time, both to travel to where the information was held, and then to find and collate it.

In those days, therefore, having access to processed information as a consultant was of value to clients as it saved them time. But the value of information has now reduced. For example, one of my clients was a market research consultancy who realised that they could no longer charge a premium for providing information which had become readily available on the internet. They had to move into consultancy to help clients in their strategic marketing decisions. The value added that the consultancy brought shifted from the information to providing advice on marketing decisions.

Similarly, management education has become widespread and so executives may well have the same, if not superior, knowledge as the consultants who serve them. Indeed, those executives may well have worked at some time in a consultancy practice.

So what value do consultants bring nowadays?

There are two perennial aspects. Firstly, there is perspective: an outsider can bring a fresh and perhaps uncluttered view to a situation that those close to it find difficult. The second is time: executives have many responsibilities and there is seldom the opportunity for them to spend uninterrupted time on addressing an issue in the way that a consultant can.

There is of course a third that can be summarised: it's not what you know, it's the way that you do it, that's important. Top consultants demonstrate excellence in the execution of their work.

Which is what this book has been all about.